FOXROCK
MISCELLANY

FOXROCK MISCELLANY

Foxrock Local History Club

edited by Myles Reid and Pádraig Laffan

The History Press Ireland

First published 2012

The History Press Ireland
119 Lower Baggot Street
Dublin 2
Ireland
www.thehistorypress.ie

British Library Cataloguing in Publication Data.
A catalogue record for this book is available from the British Library.

ISBN 978 1 84588 734 6

Typesetting and origination by The History Press

Contents

Acknowledgements

The editors are grateful to the following authors for their assistance and for their permission to publish their presentations in the Foxrock Local History series from which this miscellany is compiled, and also some extra pictures which are now compiled in this book; Liam Clare, James Scannell, Dr Brian P. Kennedy, Brian Mac Aongusa, the late Brendan Reynolds, Dr Ted Farrell, Seán Quinn and Noelle Ryan. Members of the committee of Foxrock Local History Club also provided assistance, in planning this project and deciding various aspects of the format we should follow. The members of the subcommittee who were directly involved included Maureen Daly, and Moira Laffan. Liam Clare gave much good advice and very expert assistance over a range of issues. We are grateful to Aoife Crowley for the picture of the old carriages outside Connolly's Pub, which became our cover picture, and to Ann, and Jimmy Chadwick for a picture of the old Post Office at Foxrock. Thanks also to Ronan Colgan of History Press who provided much good advice and guidance in getting the project up and running and other unnamed staff of History Press who read a large corpus of local history material from the Foxrock collection to make this selection.

Introduction

Foxrock and the South County Dublin area surrounding it making up the Half Barony of Rathdown, is a place rich in history both modern and ancient. It is from here, and occasionally further afield, that Foxrock Local History Club has drawn local history topics over the last thirty years.

Often research stretching out over many months has gone into preparing material for lectures and presentations at the public meetings. Much of this content involves people and sources that have passed away with time.

To preserve this valuable archive of wonderful local history, the club have, over the years produced a large collection of small booklets comprising an outstanding selections of these talks . The printed version of these presentations often contains more material than could be fitted into the tight time slot of the talk. This book delves into the Foxrock collection to produce inside one cover an eclectic miscellany of historical information. The topics are presented as originally given, with no attempt to update references or change the author's view as it was at the time of the presentation of the material. Hence, there may be a reference to Foxrock Railway station as 'Now unfortunately abandoned …' whereas it is, alas, in the present time vanished. It is therefore worth noting the date of presentation of the topic given after the author's name.

Dip in for a particular aspect of a story or a short read in a spare few minutes, but beware you may find it hard to put down!

This compilation contains ten topics from the Foxrock collection, ranging from the latter part of the 1700s through to the Second World War.

One will find 'The Pirates ... ' who ended up hanged in chains on the Muglins Rock as a grim warning to all sailors, also the great engineer William Dargan of Mount Anville. The local railways themselves paved the way for the great period of sea bathing and sea baths. We almost got another local railway 'The Dundrum Foxrock and Kingstown Junction Railway.' Read how it might have changed our locality, and indeed the current local rail and Luas lines of our city.

The creation of Foxrock on a green field site, and the lives of its many great characters are remembered, including the great Samuel Beckett. There are also the people and times of Cornelscourt village as portrayed in the early 20th century diary of a local shop owner.

There is the adventure the early days of aviation and even the first passenger flight in Ireland.

The shaky and dangerous handover to Irish government is chronicled, with a local shooting, and the perilous days of the Second World War with German spy Hermann Goertz.

This book will reward a casual dip or a full read of any of its stories.

Myles Reid and Pádraig Laffan, 2012

1

Those Magnificent Men in their Flying Machines – at Leopardstown

by Liam Clare (1981)

Ireland's Introduction to Aviation

> There was a remarkable scene at Foxrock railway station
> during Mr Drexel's flight. A crowded train from Dublin
> had just stopped at the station. The passengers tumbled out
> *en masse* to see the flying man, of whom they had a good
> view ... They stood on the platform and swarmed on the
> bridge, and as Drexel passed a second time, they raised a
> loud cheer. It was some time before the empty train could
> be filled up again and the passengers swept on their way.

This report from the *Freeman's Journal* of Monday 29
August 1910, illustrates the novelty of aeroplanes and
the excitement generated by flying during the first
Leopardstown air meet. Man was still in the first decade
of flight in 'heavier-than-air' machines, and people were
seeing the manmade phenomenon for the first time.

But Leopardstown may have got its first glimpse of
flying man much earlier – on 17 June 1785 to be precise.

A Dr Potain, a Frenchman living in Dublin, announced his intention of crossing the Irish Sea by balloon and gave notice to all 'fishing vessels and sea boats' to watch out for him as the balloon would 'probably go with the wind'. It did, but unfortunately for Dr Potain the wind came from the wrong direction. It carried him from his launching pad at Marlborough Green, Dublin, in a southerly direction, towards Wicklow, where he crashed near Powerscourt. This course would have taken him directly over the Leopardstown area.

Returning to the twentieth century and 'heavier-than-air' machines, many will know that the first flight took place at Kitty Hawk, North Carolina, on 17 December 1903. Orville Wright flew a distance of 120 feet (36 metres) at a height of 10 feet (3 metres). This history-making event did not even make the headlines of the day!

Progress during the first few years of the air age was painfully slow. The Wrights suspended their flights from 1905 to 1908; the first European flight was not made till 1906. As late as 1906, *The Times* of London stated that 'artificial aviation' was dangerous and doomed to failure for 'engineering reasons'.

The year of 'the Great Take Off' was 1909: the Channel was crossed by Bleriot; the first race was held in France; Britain held meetings at Blackpool and Doncaster; the first Irish flight took place on the last day of the year, when Harry Ferguson flew his homemade aeroplane at Dromore, County Down. Also, on 5 November in that year, the Irish Aero Club was formed.

The Air Show of 1910

The first attempt by the Aero Club to hold an air show – during Punchestown week in 1910 – failed through lack of subscriptions. The second fundraising appeal was more successful, and a programme for the inaugural meeting of the club was published. The cover showed Killiney Bay from the Hill, with four or five primitive aeroplanes cruising in various directions. The venue was stated as 'Leopardstown Park Racecourse' and the dates were given as Monday and Tuesday, 29 and 30 August 1910. Three aviators would participate, flying two biplanes and one monoplane, and passengers would be carried. The band of 1st Battalion Rifle Brigade would entertain the crowd and ample space would be provided for motor cars.

On 25 August, the aeroplanes began to arrive by boat, in crates, at the North Wall. One newspaper described a horse-drawn removal van trundling up Grafton Street and Harcourt Street covered with waterproof cloths. The van was labelled 'aeroplane' and bore the name 'Bleriot'. Hangars were being erected at Leopardstown by the local firm of J.S. Mason, and one plane which was damaged in transit was repaired by mechanics and by workmen from T. & C. Martin Ltd, of North Wall. Biplanes at the time cost £1,000 and monoplanes £850 (including £500 for the engine). While often damaged, they could be easily repaired. The three aviators also arrived a few days in advance of the opening day.

Captain Bertram Dickson had been an artillery officer during the Boer War. He learned to fly in a few days, and his speciality was gliding with the engine out. At Leopardstown he had a Farman biplane. He stayed

The official programme of the 1910 airshow.

with his friend Colonel Courtenay at Eaton Square, Monkstown.

Cecil Grace was born in Chile of Irish-American parents. By August 1910, he had one year's experience of flying, including many crashes. He also brought a Farman biplane to Leopardstown. He stayed with his cousin Sir Valentine Grace at Boley House, which occupied the lands where Rory O'Connor Park has since been built. A month after the Leopardstown meeting, Cecil Grace was lost on a flight over the English Channel during a dense fog.

J. Armstrong Drexel was the best known of the three aviators. He was an American citizen living in Europe and specialised in breaking altitude records. He brought two Bleriot monoplanes to Dublin, one of which could carry a passenger. He checked in at the Hibernian Hotel.

Meanwhile, work was in progress on preparing the race-course. The rails were taken down and telegraph wires were removed. *The Freeman* reported, 'to stop those who wish to see but do not wish to pay, a large force of police has been requisitioned and screens erected along the railway'.

In the advance publicity, the show was presented to the public, not as a prize competition, but as an exhibition by the best pilots and machines to introduce the science of aviation to Ireland.

The first flight took place on Sunday 28 August 1910 — the day before the meeting. Drexel was invited to lunch by Lord Powerscourt and planned to fly there. Lord Powerscourt cut down some trees on his demesne to enable Drexel to land. Drexel took off at 1.30 p.m. and quickly rose to 300 feet (90 metres). After five minutes or so he decided the weather was too blustery to attempt the 7-mile (11-kilometre) flight to Powerscourt, so he returned to land and travelled by car. This was the flight which caused such excitement among the railway passengers at Foxrock railway station.

Dublin awoke on the opening day of the air meeting to overcast skies and heavy showers. They read the fears of Mr Mason of Dame Street, the weather expert, who said, 'I think the barometer is going up too quickly – I would be better pleased if it were more gradual and had taken a couple of days to rise, instead of one day.' Yet there was a clearance at noon and a gentle south-east wind sprang up.

Despite the dull start, the *Evening Herald* was able – in a story datelined 'Aerodrome, Leopardstown, Monday' – to report, 'after that hour enormous crowds streamed towards the course in all conceivable modes of conveyance from the ostentatious twenty-horse-power motor car to the humble and less expeditious dog cart'. The Dublin and South Eastern Railway ran a shuttle train service from Dublin and Bray and special trains from more distant stations.

All newspapers reported record crowds. *The Freeman* said that by three o'clock the crowd present could only be matched by the Horse Show. It continued, 'The stands and lawns were occupied by the nobility and gentry and the ladies came in the most fashionable costumes.' This latter point was not endorsed by *The Irish Times*, which reported:

Quite a number of ladies assembled at the Leopardstown Course yesterday afternoon intense with excitement to watch the wonderful flying, although many were afraid of accidents and did not venture. The morning was not promising and the meeting from the point of view of fashion was rather disappointing. Some very smart costumes were seen, but the majority, mayhap due to the anticipated wet day, were quite ordinary. Coats and skirts, long fur coats and wraps were seen but the only item of interest was the millenary. Large hats with aeroplane wings have come for the autumn, and very becoming they look in black and white, grey and brighter colours to contrast or tone with the costume. Much black was worn yesterday and the relief in the brilliant *chapeaux* was charming. Most of the new coats and semi-hobble skirts are carried out in various tints of peach and, with large black hats and black boas, are the thing of the moment. So scattered, however, was the meeting yesterday that it was with difficulty that the dainty costumes came into view.

Everyone who was anyone attended the meeting, including the Lord Lieutenant and his wife, the Countess of Aberdeen, Mr Justice Wylie, Sir Horace Plunkett and Mr H.E. Perrin, secretary of the Aero Club of Great Britain. The Pembroke Fire Brigade were present with 'horses and water engines'; St John's Ambulance Brigade came from St James's Gate; the Dolphin Hotel did the catering, and 300 pressmen covered the event.

There was an entrance for cars and motorcycles at the Stillorgan end near the 5s enclosure, while the road for bicycles and pedestrians led to the 2s 6d gate.

The 5s secured a spectator access to the stands and closer access to the planes; for half a crown one stood in a mile-long (1.5 kilometre) enclosure which ran from the Stillorgan end to Foxrock railway station.

One man who objected strongly to paying was a Mr Lane Joynt, a member of Leopardstown Club. As a member, he was entitled to a free entry to the course during the currency of his membership, together with free entry for two ladies and his motor car. Membership passes were withdrawn for the days of the air meeting and Mr Lane Joynt sought an injunction against Leopardstown Club Ltd to secure free entry. As the courts were in recess, the 'vacation judge' held a special sitting of court. The judge said that to bring a judge to court on a vacation like this (Friday of Horse Show week) for a case like this was 'very little short of an outrage'. He held that the plaintiff was not being refused admission but would merely have to pay a maximum of £1 17s 6d. He therefore dismissed the case.

Others avoided payment by less drastic means: they congregated on roads and fields along the railway; they perched on branches of trees; they clambered onto the roofs of railway carriages; they climbed the ladders on signal posts; crowds even gathered on the Three Rock Mountain and Killiney Hill.

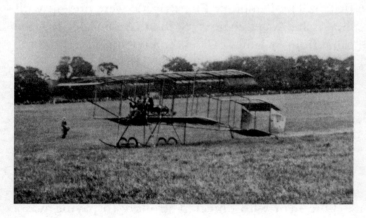

First passenger flight in Ireland, 1910.

Those present at the air meeting were to witness eight flights. In the morning, Cecil Grace made an unofficial trial flight of two circuits which one newspaper described as 'pretty'. As he passed over a group of trees he startled a colony of rooks, who rose in the air with him and circled around the aeroplane 'in evident wonder and dismay'. The rooks followed the aeroplane for a time and then disappeared.

As the crowds waited for the official start of the meeting, rumours spread around the grounds that a British aviator, Robert Loraine, known to be waiting at Holyhead for favourable weather, would be landing at Leopardstown during the meeting after the first successful Irish Sea flight. Field glasses scanned the sky to the east in anticipation of his appearance but to no avail. He did not arrive.

At 3 p.m. there was a parade of the three aeroplanes from the hangars to the starting point. Grace led the trio, followed by Dickson and Drexel in that order. Soon Grace was up again. He headed towards the railway station, then back over the stand, away to the south over to Ballycorus, and then reappeared over the station at 200 feet (60 metres) before coming to land.

Drexel's turn came next. He did five circuits of the course, swooping down from time to time. He landed after eleven minutes.

Dickson's plane hopped about 200 yards (180 metres), before he brought it to a halt. He then had it taken away for overhaul.

Following further flights by Grace and Drexel, the latter heading first towards the Three Rock Mountain and then Killiney, Grace took up his passenger plane. He carried Mr Desmond Arthur of Ennis, County Clare, the first aeroplane passenger in Ireland, for about 600 yards (550 metres). Arthur had to walk back; Grace flew, stating he would have gone further only for the heavy weight.

After Drexel 'flew high' – up to 1,000 feet (300 metres) – Dickson finally flew a circuit of the course and landed 'gracefully'. He had had his aeroplane overhauled and had changed the petrol. He alleged that someone may have tampered with the machine overnight.

The aviators agreed that Leopardstown was 'nice' for exhibitions but not for record breaking. They felt the currents were too tricky, due to variations in the strength and direction of the wind. The crowd was well satisfied, having come face to face with the new wonder of the world.

That night, the Corinthian Club held a dinner in the Gresham Hotel in honour of the three aviators. *The Freeman* reported:

> After an excellent repast had been partaken of, the loyal toasts were honoured at the call of the chairman. Then Sir Charles Cameron proposed a toast to the airmen. A capital musical programme followed and Mrs Power O'Donoghue recited an original poem, 'Ode to the Airmen'.

The second day, in contrast to the first, was a day of high winds and low, short flights. The Dublin Bread Company had offered £50 for the first aviator to fly from Leopardstown around the dome of their premises in Sackville Street and back to the course, but the weather precluded the accepting of this challenge.

The attendance was down compared with the previous day, particularly in the cheaper 2s 6d enclosure, but the unofficial attendance was up, as news got around that the meeting was worth seeing and, moreover, that it could be seen free of charge from outside the grounds.

Dublin's *Evening Herald* reported enormous crowds on Torquay Road, Westminster Road, Foxrock Golf Club, Foxrock railway station, the Three Rock Mountains and Killiney Hill. They hardly saw a thing, however, because the winds caused the aeroplanes to keep low and inside the course, behind the screens. The super-optimistic did not travel to Foxrock at all, but climbed Nelson's Pillar, whose management reported a record attendance despite the 'house full' notices and the consequent turning away of many potential clients.

The event was one of short flights only; Drexel did not fly at all; there was no flying till 4 p.m. Then Grace took off and made two circuits of the course at 300 feet. The vast crowds cheered him on his second round. From then until 7 p.m., he amused the spectators with an exhibition of 'hopping'. He took up passengers at a charge of £10 per head, one of whom, the first female passenger in Ireland, was referred to in the papers under the pseudonym of 'Miss Smith'. Just before 7 p.m., Dickson flew around the course – his sole contribution to the day's proceedings.

Next day, a flight over the city from Leopardstown to the Phoenix Park was planned by a Mr McArdle, flying Drexel's plane. This flight, too, had to be cancelled, due to strong winds.

To the relief of the persons who had made the meeting possible by guaranteeing the organisers against a loss of up to £2,000, the profit, after takings were counted and expenses calculated, came to £400.

Robert Loraine, who was rumoured to be flying the Irish Sea on the first day of the meeting, actually made his attempt twelve days later. He took off from Holyhead safely but as he approached the Bailey Lighthouse on Howth, his engine cut out and he had to ditch in the sea. He swam ashore, where he was met by members of a new, and as yet unnamed, cycling club. The club still exists under the title of Loraine Cycling Club.

Flight magazine ended its report on the meeting as follows: 'Indeed I shall not be surprised, if next year Ireland does not hold a point-to-point aeroplane race, as for example, between Dublin and Belfast, or the other way about.'

The Great Air Race of 1912

This forecast was not too far wrong, for two years later the Irish Aero Club announced a Dublin to Belfast and back air race – Leopardstown to Balmoral and back, to be precise – for 7 September 1912. The journey of 110 miles (180 kilometres) between the two cities was expected to take ninety minutes, while a compulsory thirty-minute break was to be made at Balmoral.

Again, the aeroplanes arrived at North Wall, but this time they were towed backwards to Leopardstown, the tailplanes being held on the backs of motor cars. One car was punctured at the Custom House and a huge crowd gathered to view the spectacle.

A programme was again published in advance, carrying the same cover picture of aeroplanes over Killiney Bay as appeared on the 1910 programme. Although advance publicity mentioned seventeen competitors, the programme only listed eleven. The prizes offered were a £300 first prize and a £75 second prize, together with up to £40 expenses for each competitor to be taken out of any net profit. The rules permitted landing *en route*.

To keep the crowds at Leopardstown entertained while the aeroplanes were on the journey, two bands were engaged; the band of the Metropolitan Police and that of the Royal Irish Constabulary. In addition, a French aviator, a Mr Salmet, was recruited to provide a flying display. The prices were slightly down on the 1910 meeting, being 2s or 4s 6d, plus an extra 2s 6d admission to the aeroplane enclosure. Pembroke Fire Brigade undertook to be in attendance with their 'chemical fire engine'. St John's Ambulance Brigade also agreed to attend. The Dolphin Hotel were the caterers, as in 1910, and were advertised as providing hot and cold lunches, teas, ices and wines. A huge notice board was erected to give progress reports, while 'telegraphic and telephonic communication' was established with Belfast. As an added safety precaution, RIC barracks, lighthouses, lightships and coastguard stations were charged to be on the lookout for the aviators.

The Irish Times described the race as a fiasco — a fairly accurate assessment. Initially, seventeen aviators were expected; eleven were named in the programme; four turned up at Leopardstown; only two planes got away.

The gates at Leopardstown Racecourse opened at 11 a.m., as the race was due to start at 1.30 p.m. A stream of cars and many special trains brought the crowds to Leopardstown. One newspaper reported that many spectators took the tram to Temple Hill and, to save money, walked up Newtownpark Avenue.

The gentry were present in force, as they had been in 1910. The Earl and Countess of Mayo, Lord Fingall and son, Lord and Lady Powerscourt with a party of friends, and Sir Horace Plunkett, with several friends, were among the crowd.

As on the previous occasion, vast numbers watched from vantage points outside the course, but because of the nature of the great air race, the view points were more scattered than two years previously: the north shore of Dublin Bay, Howth Head, Killiney Hill, the Bull Wall, Merrion/Sandymount Strand and Herbert Park. The sky watchers waited for two hours in vain, unaware that the notice board at Leopardstown indicated that the start would be delayed due to bad weather at Belfast.

Mr Salmet took off at 2.30 p.m. for what had been described as 'an exhibition of spectacular flying'. Due to a strong wind, he flew at a low level doing figures of eight east of the railway and over Carrickmines for about ten minutes. Then he landed and put the aeroplane away.

At 2.30 p.m., the notice board indicated that the race would be shortened to the Leopardstown–Balmoral leg only; at 3.30 p.m. it promised a start in ten minutes but a drizzle began to fall and the planes were put back into their hangars.

At 4.25 p.m. the first flyer took off. He was Mr H.J.D. Astley, described in the programme as an 'excellent specimen of British sportsman'. His Bleriot monoplane headed over Stillorgan and was soon merely a dot in the sky.

Two minutes after Astley set off, James Valentine was called. He was described in the official programme as 'one of the best-known pilots in the world'. He took off from the racecourse 'slowly' in his Morane monoplane and was gone.

Mr Desmond Arthur,
1912.

At 4.37 p.m., Mr Desmond Arthur, who became the first air passenger in Ireland when he flew with Grace at the 1910 meeting, tried to take off in his Bleriot monoplane. He failed to raise the plane, came back to earth and skidded to a halt just short of the press tent. A wheel was punctured but nevertheless he made a further unsuccessful attempt on the flat tyre before giving up.

Finally, at 4.48 p.m., Lieutenant J.C. Porte, 'son of the late Vicar of Bandon', took off in his Deperdussin monoplane and headed towards the mountains before appearing again beyond Stillorgan. He returned to Leopardstown after five minutes, complaining that he could not cope with the blustery wind.

The national anthem, 'God Save the King', was then played and proceedings at Leopardstown drew to a close.

Meanwhile, Astley flew across Dublin Bay at 1,500 feet (500 metres), rose to 2,000 feet (600 metres) over Sutton and, looking ahead, could see the Mournes. As he climbed to 5,000 feet (1,500 metres), he found himself being blown out to sea. From 7 miles (11 kilometres) offshore he struggled back towards land, crossed the coast at Dunany Point beyond Clogher Head, and caught up on Valentine, who had previously passed him. He headed towards Dundalk, but after fifty-one minutes in the air, realised he couldn't reach Balmoral. He therefore headed back south. Eventually he landed in a field near Drogheda. His arrival caused great excitement; thousands of spectators paid 3 *d* each for entry to the field to see the flying machine.

Valentine just cleared the trees surrounding the course as he headed towards Dublin Bay. He got a fine view of Kingstown, then passed over Sutton and Lambay Island, and overtook Astley. From Clogher Head he kept in to land and saw the Mourne Mountains ahead, shrouded in mist. About 3 miles (5 kilometres) beyond Dundalk, he experienced severe buffeting from the gusty winds and decided that he had no choice but to seek a spot where he could land. In the mountainous areas of North Louth and South Armagh, there were few suitable landing fields, but he took a chance and landed in a small field just outside Newry.

Next morning, when he returned to the field, he found the aeroplane surrounded by a canvas screen erected on four upturned carts. Ten men with sticks stood on guard duty outside. They were charging 3 *d* admission. Valentine was asked by a woman to pay for damage to the crops, which he claimed were non-existent. He told her to seek a percentage of the threepences being collected.

Aviators, 1910. From left (in front): Captain Bertram Dixon, J. Armstrong Drexel and Cecil Grace.

The £300 first prize was split evenly between Astley and Valentine; the £75 prize was divided into £50 for Porte and £25 for Arthur. All four competitors got £40 expenses from the profits.

If the event that afternoon at Leopardstown was unsatisfactory, it was positively disastrous at Balmoral. The weather was overcast, wet and blustery and not an aeroplane was glimpsed all afternoon. Many people demanded their money back but this was refused. However, charity air displays were held on the next two weekends. During the latter show, Astley's plane went out of control and he was killed.

Aeronautics magazine had warned, before the race, that Leopardstown was quite unsuitable for the purpose because of air currents, and called it 'a certain death trap' in a south-west wind. With this reputation, it is perhaps not surprising that Leopardstown was not chosen as one of the airfields for the Dublin area during the First Wold War. These were located instead at Collinstown (now Dublin Airport), Baldonnel (now Casement) and Tallaght, where some of the huts are still visible at Belgard Road.

Wartime Forced Landings at Leopardstown

But Leopardstown Racecourse was to figure twice during the Second World War as a site chosen for forced landings.

On 25 May 1941, five Bristol Beaufighters of RAF Coastal Command ran into bad weather and heavy fog while on the last leg of a flight from Malta via Gibraltar to Cornwall. They lost contact with each other; three made it to various British airfields; one ditched in the sea; the fifth emerged from the clouds, saw the level expanse of Leopardstown Racecourse and landed 'wheels up'. The propeller was bent and the body was damaged. Irish Army Air Corps engineers dismantled the plane and took it away. The crew were returned to Britain as they were not on an operational flight.

Nearly three years later, on 22 February 1944, two C-47s of the United States Army Air Force were seen circling over Balbriggan at noon, obviously seeking a place to land. One pilot eventually landed at Leopardstown without damaging his aircraft. The crew of three or four were delivering the plane from the factory in the United States to England as part of the build-up of war *materiel* prior to D-Day. They had flown via Gander, Greenland, Iceland and Prestwick and were on the last stage of the flight when they found themselves short of fuel. Because of the nature of their flight, the crew were allowed to refuel and take off again next day.

The area has one other link with aviation: the first successful home-built plane on the 'EI register' (that is, built in the twenty-six counties) was constructed by Michael Donoghue in his garage at Clonkeen Drive. He first flew the craft in April 1976 and is still flying high.

Finally ...

Finally, to return to the great air race. Each flier was given a message by the Lord Mayor of Dublin to deliver to the Lord Mayor of Belfast. It read:

> The Lord Mayor of Dublin takes a keen interest in the air race to Belfast. Glad to take official recognition of every means which will bring Belfast and Dublin together and lead to a better understanding between the people of the two cities. Between aeroplanes, trains and motor cars it is quite evident that we shall arrive at a time when Belfast and Dublin will in reality become one as far as opinions are concerned.

Pity the fliers never reached Belfast!

An Aviation Meeting, September 7th

The unknown there, was ramparted by hills,
That spilt their purple almost to the course,
And o'er their rim mysteriously the mist,

The white mist leaned, and to the wild things round
Breathed 'Bear with this awhile – child's play it is
That might shall sweep away and then for us
The old good silence shall be found once more.'
And slowly o'er the field men bore the corpse
That they would galvanise to seeming life –
The great mock bird, the aeroplane! Above
The wild crows in their gracious noiseless flight
Were held by pity mute – for they had seen –
Ah they had seen such great wings quiver – break
And man's poor toy drop broken to the ground.

by E. Fortesque Moresby
The Irish Review, October 1912

References and Further Reading

Newspapers
Evening Herald
Freeman's Journal
The Irish Times

Magazines and Journals
Aeronautics
Flight
Irish Life
Irish Review

Books

Byrne, Liam *History of Aviation in Ireland* (Dublin; Blackwater Press, 1980)

Villard, Henry Serrano *Contact - The Story of the Early Birds* (London; Arther Barker, 1969)

2

Shooting Incident at Westminster Road, 1922

by James Scannell (1991)

On 21 January 1919, about 200 people filed into the Mansion House in Dublin, to witness those Sinn Féin representatives who could attend declare themselves as the Assembly of Ireland – Dáil Éireann. Of the seventy-three members elected in the previous December's General Election, only twenty-seven TDs were able to be present and in this first session, which was chaired by Cathal Brugha, the Dáil issued a Declaration of Independence, sent messages of goodwill to other nations, issued its democratic programme and announced its intention of setting up its own machinery of State.

A campaign to undermine the institutions of Dublin Castle commenced and the first target to be selected for elimination was the Royal Irish Constabulary (RIC), which in 1919 was about 10,000 strong, spread over 1,200 heavily fortified barracks. As a police force, the RIC was unique in that it combined the functions of a rural gendarmerie, a civil police force and a rudimentary civil service outside the larger towns. Well armed and equipped, the RIC was spread throughout the country in small detachments within easy reach of each other in the event of serious disturbance.

On the afternoon of 21 January 1919, the military campaign in the War of Independence began at Soloheadbeg in County Tipperary, when eight members of the South Tipperary Brigade IRA ambushed two employees of the South Tipperary County Council who were in the process of conveying gelignite by cart from Tipperary town to Soloheadbeg quarry.

In the ambush, the two RIC constables acting as escort were killed, their arms taken and the gelignite seized. This incident was the first of hundreds which were to be placed under the general heading of 'outrages'.

From this date until the signing of the truce in July 1921, the RIC were exposed to a campaign of boycott, intimidation, ambush and shooting. The result was to put the RIC on the defensive, though in some cases members did resign in the face of the campaign.

By the end of 1919, the RIC had withdrawn from large areas of the countryside, and to maintain a semblance of law and order in these areas, policing was undertaken by a force known as the IRA police/'IR' police, who brought offenders before the Republican Courts which had been set up as an alternative legal system to the Crown Courts.

In 1920, as the ferocity of the fighting intensified, the British introduced two hastily recruited forces – the Black and Tans and the Auxiliaries – to combat the IRA as the British Army began to lose control of the countryside.

In 1921, the War of Independence reached a new level of ferocity, with IRA attacks on barracks and military convoys being followed by large-scale reprisals. Town centres, villages and creameries were burned down by the Black and Tans; a policy which further alienated the population and led to growing protests in Britain and America.

However, by July 1921, the military campaigns had reached stalemate, and on 22 June 1921, King George V, in a carefully worded speech at the formal opening of the Northern Ireland Parliament, asked all Irishmen 'to pause, to stretch out the hand of forbearance and conciliation, to forgive and forget and to join in making for the land they love a new era of peace, contentment and goodwill'.

An exchange of letters between de Valera and Lloyd George followed and this resulted in a meeting in the Mansion House, Dublin, on 8 July, between representatives of the IRA and the government forces, at which a truce was agreed. Under the truce, all aggressive acts and provocative displays of force by either side were to cease at 12 noon on 11 July, and there was a provision that it could be terminated by either side at seventy-two hours' notice. A body known as the Truce Liaison Committee was created to settle any disputes which arose between members of the IRA and the British government forces.

During the truce period, members of the RIC, Auxiliaries, Black and Tans, and IRA were able to mix freely, while the politicians tried to resolve the problem of independence through dialogue. Policing in many parts of the country was carried out by both the RIC, who maintained that they held their authority from Dublin Castle, and by the IR police, who maintained that they held their authority from Dáil Éireann.

In some places these forces worked together, in others they resented each other, and in others they worked independently of each other.

Offenders arrested by the IR police were usually brought before the Republican Courts, while those detained by the RIC were usually brought before the Crown Courts, which continued to function as normal.

During this period, in Bray, County Wicklow, policing of the town was carried out by both the IR police and the RIC, with both forces operating independently of each other.

On 23 November 1921, a curious incident, which the newspapers would later call 'the Bray Mystery', occurred. Four members of the IRA – William Kelly, Carrickmines, and Patrick Devlin, Timothy McCarthy and Patrick Mulvaney, all from Deansgrange – visited the licensed premises of John Ryan at Main Street, Bray, and attempted to obtain from the proprietor the sum of £500 through a combination of threats and menaces. However, before they could obtain the money, they recognised an IRA officer in the immediate vicinity and fled from the scene before they could be identified.

The incident was forgotten about, and very quickly was overshadowed by national events, with the signing of the Anglo-Irish Treaty on 6 December 1921, which granted independence with certain conditions to the territory which today comprises the Republic of Ireland.

For the RIC, as elsewhere in Ireland, the Treaty confirmed an agreement reached in London between Michael Collins and the Chief Secretary Sir Hamar Greenwood shortly after the implementation of the truce, that the RIC would have to be disbanded by whatever government was created by the final negotiated settlement, i.e. the Treaty. Quite simply, the RIC had fought against the IRA in the War of Independence and therefore were not acceptable to the Irish people as a police force. The Dublin Metropolitan Police fared better, in that it was agreed that they would be retained, though a question over the future of the notorious 'G' Division, which dealt with political matters and operated from Dublin Castle, was left unresolved.

From July to December 1921, the RIC and IR police operated in Bray independently of each other, as did the two courts. When the internees were released under the terms of the Treaty in early December, the Bray RIC maintained a low profile while the local men were accorded a heroes' welcome on their return to the town.

However, after Christmas the RIC appear to have adopted a hostile attitude towards the IR police and the Republican Court. This possibly stemmed from the fact that they knew that their days of keeping the peace were numbered, and that they would be replaced by men who only months previously had been attacking them.

About half an hour before the scheduled Monday 2 January sitting of the Republican Court in the Town Hall, a number of the RIC arrived and made their presence known, but they did not interfere with what was planned. They left after satisfying themselves that the use of the Town Hall had been authorised for this purpose, but in any event the sitting had to be cancelled due to two of the three District Justices who normally attended not being able to come, due to what was described as, 'national business'.

On 7 January, the Dáil voted on the Treaty terms, which were accepted by a margin of sixty-four 'for' and fifty-seven 'against'.

Two days later, on Monday 9 January, a curious incident occurred outside the premises of the Northern Bank on the Quinsboro Road, where the current branch of the National Irish Bank is located.

In reprisal for attacks against Catholics and Nationalists in Belfast, the IRA organised a national boycott against Northern Ireland businesses based in the Free State and on their goods which were on sale. As part of this campaign, the IR police in Bray mounted a picket outside the Northern Bank branch on Monday 9 January. The RIC were called; they asked the picket to disperse but they refused to do so. Reinforcements were sent for, and half an hour later Head Constable Taylor and six constables arrived on the scene and forced the picket to leave. Later, the picket reappeared, but this time the RIC did not intervene.

However, within twenty-four hours, an incident of a more serious nature occurred.

Around 10.30 p.m. on Tuesday 10 January, the four IRA men who had tried to obtain money from John Ryan in November returned to his premises and attempted to get him to sign a document which stated that the 23 November incident had never happened. The IR police were called but took no action and withdrew from the scene after they were convinced by the four men that they were acting in an official capacity and that their demand that John Ryan sign the document was an authorised one.

Matters between John Ryan and William Kelly, leader of the group, became very heated, and while they argued, word was sent of the ongoing incident to the RIC, who rushed in force to the scene.

Head Constable Taylor and his men arrived in the licensed premises just as Kelly was about to produce a revolver and force John Ryan to sign this declaration. Quickly, Head Constable Taylor grabbed Kelly, while a Sergeant Ryan grabbed the revolver. The subsequent search of the men revealed that Devlin had a Webley revolver, McCarthy, a Colt revolver and Mulvaney, a dagger. The four men were arrested and taken to the Bray RIC barracks where they refused to answer questions before being placed in the cells.

Word of the incident was conveyed to the Truce Liaison Office in Dublin, and the next day, Wednesday 11 January, four IRA officers were sent to Bray by motor car to resolve the incident. On arrival in the town, they went to the police barracks and sought out Head Constable Taylor. They requested permission to see the four detained men but this was denied. They decided not to take no for an answer and kept asking Head Constable Taylor that they be allowed to see the detainees. Finally, in annoyance, Head Constable Taylor arrested the four and lodged them in the cells.

Arrangements were made for a special sitting of the Bray Petty Sessions. This took place on Thursday 12 January before Mr Jasper White, RM. Kelly, Mulvaney, Devlin and McCarthy were formally charged by Head Constable Taylor:

a) that on 23 November 1921, at Main Street, Bray, defendants did unlawfully by threats and menaces endeavour to obtain a sum of £500 from John Ryan with intent to defraud, and

b) that on 10 January 1922, at Main Street, Bray, defendants did unlawfully by threats and menaces endeavour to obtain from the said John Ryan, a written declaration to the effect that they had not committed the above offence.

Evidence concerning the events of 23 November 1921 and 10 January 1922 was heard from John Ryan and details of arrest was given by Head Constable Taylor.

In response to questions from the RM, Mr Jasper White, the men were evasive in their answers and unco-operative. At the end of the hearing, the four defendants were remanded into the custody of Head Constable Taylor for a period of seven days.

The four IRA Truce Liaison Officers who had been arrested by Head Constable Taylor were brought into court and were discharged when Head Constable Taylor indicated that he had no charges against them.

The four prisoners were returned to the cells in the RIC barracks while the four Truce Liaison Officers returned to Dublin.

The IRA realised that the four men were not going to be released through the efforts of the Truce Liaison Office, which had been created to resolve this type of dispute, and they put in hand plans to release the four men.

It was accepted that the Bray RIC barracks could not be attacked, as this was well defended by the RIC.

It was also accepted that such an incident would be a most serious truce violation and would create problems, rather than solving them. The final option was to attempt to release them while on the way from Bray to Dublin if they were still remanded at the next sitting of the Bray Court.

The seven days remand was to allow the RIC to carry out further inquiries, but during this period they do not appear to have contacted the IR police to find out what the accused had told them and instead spent the time preparing their case against them.

The case against the four men resumed before Mr Jasper White, RM, in Bray Courthouse on Thursday 19 January 1922. Principal witness against the four was Head Constable Taylor, who confirmed his testimony given at the previous hearing.

The four accused refused to recognise the court; they would not remove their headgear and objected to being handcuffed and treated as common criminals.

When Head Constable Taylor had given his evidence, the four were allowed to cross-examine him.

Kelly made the point of informing the court that they had been subjected to rough treatment when brought to the Bray RIC barracks and that he had been assaulted by a member of the force. Mr White disallowed this point on the basis that it bore no relavance to the matter before them but said that he could press charges against the RIC should he wish to do so.

Mulvaney said that at the time of the 10 January incident, he had informed the police that they were IRA men on duty and that they had documents with them to confirm this.

While Head Constable Taylor denied that he knew that they were IRA men on duty, he confirmed that they had told him this. He also confirmed that the four men had surrendered their weapons when asked to do so.

Mulvaney then asked Taylor if he had a book with a statement in it and if so, that this statement should be admitted in evidence. In reply, Taylor indicated that he did have a book, which he found on Kelly.

Mulvaney then protested against being handcuffed and being treated as common criminals, 'If we have done wrong we claim the right as soldiers of the Irish Republic to be tried by our own officers.'

The final comment was made by McCarthy, who said that the matter could be explained if the police got in touch with their own officers. He concluded by saying that they were being humiliated by being brought before the court.

On the basis of the evidence presented, Mr White found in favour of the RIC and remanded the four prisoners. The RIC then began to make the necessary arrangements to bring the four men to Mountjoy Gaol until their case came before the courts again.

News of the remand provided the IRA with the opportunity to bring into operation their plan to release the four.

It was expected that the men would travel by road to Dublin, so two groups of men took up positions covering the two likely routes the RIC would use. One group stationed themselves at Westminster Road, just beyond Cornelscourt Village, while the other possibly waited down at the Deansgrange end of the Clonkeen Road.

At that time, much of this area would have consisted of fields and tracks, with only a few houses here and there. Around 3.30 p.m., in the failing light of a January evening, the four men were brought from the RIC barracks, where they had remained after that day's court appearance, and placed in what was described as a 'charabanc' surrounded by an RIC escort with Head Constable Taylor in charge.

The vehicle followed the old Bray–Dublin Road as far as Cabinteely village. As the car passed through Cabinteely village, three Crossley tenders of Black and Tans from Wexford who had halted at the Cabinteely RIC barracks while on the way to Gormanstown, County Dublin, for disbandment, were preparing to depart to resume their journey, and they decided to follow the RIC vehicle.

At the fork in the road beyond Cabinteely village, the RIC vehicle turned left and followed the road up through Cornelscourt village and headed towards Dublin via Stillorgan. This was right into the hands of the IRA ambush party which was lying in wait at Westminster Road. To ensure that no one would get hurt, all pedestrians had been advised to take cover and to keep away.

As the RIC vehicle approached Westminster Road, suddenly a Ford motor car was pushed across the road, forcing the RIC to brake sharply. Before those inside could react to events, the vehicle was surrounded by members of the IRA ambush party, who released the four men and made the RIC members throw away their weapons. The ambush party were in the process of making their withdrawal when the three Crossley tenders full of Black and Tans arrived on the scene. They dismounted, and joining with the RIC, pursued the IRA members over the surrounding fields. During the chase, shots were fired, but the early evening twilight made accurate shooting impossible, so neither side sustained any casualties.

Efforts by the RIC to use their own vehicle in the pursuit of the escapees and their rescuers had to be aborted when it was discovered that the rear axle was broken. A quick check of the Ford car used to barricade the road revealed that there was no petrol in its tank.

The ambush party and those rescued were able to flee the scene very quickly, and the only consolation for the RIC was that they were able to detain a young man who injured his hand on some barbed wire. The injured man was brought by the RIC to their depot in Dublin, where his injuries were treated, and he was released without charge the next day. The RIC submitted a full report on the incident and that was the end of it.

The RIC members returned to Bray, where they spent their remaining time dealing with outstanding matters on hand, and they were formally relieved on 15 March 1922, when policing of the town was taken over by members of the South Dublin Brigade IRA.

Cabinteely RIC barracks was taken over by the same unit on Wednesday, 16 February 1922. They in turn handed the barracks over to representatives of the provisional government on Sunday, 19 February 1922.

References and Further Reading

Books
Bowyer Bell, J., *The Secret Army* (London, 1970).
Brady, Conor, *Guardians of the Peace* (Dublin, 1974).
The Educational Co., *Ireland* 3 (Dublin, 1972).
Kee, Robert, *The Green Flag, Vol.* 3, (London, 1987).
Kenny, Michael, *The Road to Independence* (Dublin, 1991).
Younger, Carton, *Ireland's Civil War* (London, 1982).

Newspapers
Evening Mail (Dublin)
Evening Telegraph (Dublin)
The Wicklow Newsletter
The Wicklow People

3

Dr Hermann Goertz: A German Spy in South County Dublin

by Brian P. Kennedy (1989)

After the First World War, it was an axiom of the German Secret Service that the key to sabotage and espionage operations in Great Britain was to be found in Ireland.

This view was shared by Admiral Wilhelm Canaris, Head of the German Secret Service, until 1945, when he was hanged for his part in the attempted assassination of Hitler. On the wall opposite Canaris's desk in Berlin hung a portrait of Colonel Nicolai, the Kaiser's Intelligence Chief who had organised the mission of Sir Roger Casement to Ireland.

Canaris's colleague Major-General Erwin von Lahousen de Vivremont was keen to establish links with the Irish Republican Army when it began a bombing campaign in Britain in January 1939. A German officer, Oskar Pfaus, was sent to Dublin and made contact with Seán Russell, Chief of Staff of the IRA, and with James O'Donovan, Director of Chemicals of the Old IRA during the War of Independence and architect of the 1939 bombing campaign in Britain – the so-called 'S-Plan' ('S' for sabotage).

In February, April and August 1939, O'Donovan made visits to Germany and had discussions with the German Secret Service about the supply of arms and wireless sets to Ireland in the event of war, and about arrangements for contacts with German agents. Meanwhile, dozens of explosions orchestrated by the IRA took place in Britain. Bombs exploded in letter boxes, underground stations, cars, shops and hotels. The IRA aimed to create an atmosphere of terror in Britain.

The Second World War began in September 1939. The Taoiseach, Éamon de Valera, declared that Ireland would be a neutral country for the duration of what would be known officially as the Emergency. It became necessary to prevent the IRA from continuing its bombing campaign in Britain lest it jeopardise Ireland's neutrality. The bombing campaign inflicted material damage only at first, but following the deaths of five people in an explosion at Coventry, the British Government brought extreme pressure to bear on the Irish Government to act against the IRA. Eventually, an IRA raid on the Magazine Fort in the Phoenix Park on 23 December 1939 prompted the Irish Government to pass an Emergency Powers Act which allowed the use of exceptional powers of internment of IRA members and the execution of convicted IRA bombers.

All this activity was monitored by the German Secret Service via radio messages transmitted by the IRA. The Germans began to make arrangements to send a number of agents – that is, 'spies' – to Ireland to establish contact with the IRA. Most of the agents despatched to Ireland, of whom there were a dozen approximately, were arrested quickly by the Irish defence and security forces. All were unsuccessful in furthering Germany's war aims. The least unsuccessful, and the agent who operated for the longest period before being arrested, was Dr Hermann Goertz. Most of his time in Ireland was spent in the area of South County Dublin.

Hermann Goertz was born in Lübeck in 1890. He was the son of a wealthy and distinguished lawyer. Following family tradition, Goertz studied law. During the First World War he served in Russia and was wounded at Christmas 1914. He received the Iron Cross for valour and enlisted in the Luftwaffe as a reconnaissance officer, and later as an interrogation officer. At the time of the Armistice, Goertz clashed with Captain Hermann Goering and persuaded him not to set fire to German planes rather than surrender them. Goertz argued sensibly that this would only mean heavier reparations for an already defeated Germany.

Goertz returned to his law practice after the war. He specialised in international law, in which he held a doctorate. He married Ellen Aschenborn, the daughter of a German admiral. Goertz was a cultured man, an enthusiastic sportsman, gifted at mathematics and an excellent hill walker. In 1935, after Hitler came to power, conscription was reintroduced in Germany and Goertz rejoined the Luftwaffe. He volunteered to supply proof of his belief that the Royal Air Force in Britain was establishing a fleet of large bombers. Goertz was sent to England and, on the pretext of researching a book, he toured the south-east of the country, making studies of numerous RAF bases. A landlady in one place in which he stayed became suspicious about his activities, reported him to the police, and some time later, Goertz was arrested. His trial caused a sensation in Britain. He was sentenced to four years penal servitude for spying.

During his stay in Parkhurst Prison, Goertz came into contact with a number of IRA prisoners who had been sentenced for their parts in the bombing campaign in Britain. Goertz had visited Ireland in 1927 and the beauty of the country's landscape had impressed him. He had also made some acquaintances in the Clan na Gael movement in the United States when attending international law conferences and during periods of research there.

Goertz was released from prison in 1939 and returned to Germany. Following five months' sick leave, he resumed duty as a German agent. He suggested to his superiors that the IRA in Britain could be used as spies for Germany. This did not impress the German High Command, but they were interested in the idea that the IRA could be used to create troubles in Ulster which would destabilise Britain. It was decided that Goertz would be sent on a mission to Ireland as an intelligence officer (he disliked the title 'spy'), charged with liaising with the IRA, making the IRA more interested in Northern Ireland, and preparing the way for spying and sabotage operations there. Goertz was trained in sabotage tactics and studied Irish affairs with the help of a number of Irishmen living in Germany, including the novelist Francis Stuart, who was a lecturer in Anglo-Irish literature at Berlin University.

The code name for the plan to parachute Goertz into Ireland was 'Operation Mainau'. Mainau is an island on Lake Constance and was chosen presumably because it was a suitable codeword for the 'Emerald Isle'.

On the night of 5 May 1940, a black Heinkel flew over County Meath and two parachutes floated landward. Goertz landed near Ballivor. It was raining and visibility was poor. He was unable to locate the second parachute which was to deliver his wireless set. Thus, from the beginning of his mission, Goertz was dogged by disaster. Curiously, Goertz had insisted that he should wear his full military uniform (so that if caught he would be charged as a German officer). On consideration, however, he decided that it would be unwise to walk through the Irish countryside in this attire, so he hid it along with his parachute. Instead, he wore his breeches, riding boots, a pullover and a black beret. He retained a considerable sum of English and American currency and, out of sentiment, his German war medals. He also had a phial of potassium cyanide which he proposed to take if he was captured and tortured to make him reveal secrets.

Goertz had been instructed to make contact with Jim O'Donovan but first to go to the home of Francis Stuart's wife, Iseult, at Laragh Castle in County Wicklow. Iseult Stuart, a daughter of Maud Gonne MacBride and a sister of Seán MacBride, was not expecting Goertz. He had to convince her that he knew her husband and that he was a German officer. Goertz, aged fifty, hungry and dishevelled after four days walking from Meath, did not look very convincing. In any event, Iseult Stuart sent him to bed for the day and went to Dublin City to buy a suit of clothes for her visitor. That night, a car arrived without warning at the house and a frightened Goertz fled out the door. But the driver of the car was Jim O'Donovan, and after locating Goertz, he took him to his house, Florenceville, at Shankill, County Dublin. Jim O'Donovan did not know how to explain Goertz's presence to his children and his maid. He explained the situation to his wife, Monty (a sister of the patriot Kevin Barry), and she prepared a bed for Goertz in the garage.

For the next few days, Goertz spent his time wandering about in the orchard. On the third night, four IRA men arrived and asked Goertz to go with them and to bring his money. They took him to the house of Stephen Held, Villa Konstanz, on the Templeogue Road. Stephen Held had been sent to Germany by Jim O'Donovan and had arrived there on the same day that Goertz had left for Ireland. In Held's house, Goertz met Stephen Hayes, who had taken over from Seán Russell as Chief of Staff of the IRA. Goertz discussed the IRA's activities with Hayes but he was not impressed by the organisation. He was upset when the IRA failed to locate his uniform from where he had hidden it in Meath, although his parachute was recovered.

Laragh Castle as it is today.

On 25 May 1940, the police arrived at Held's house. Goertz was immediately rushed out the back door and he jumped over the garden wall and fled. Meanwhile, the police entered the house and searched it. In an upstairs room, they found a typewriter, a file with details about Irish harbours, bridges and airfields, a parachute, a wireless transmitter and receiver, a safe containing 18,500 American dollars, some German war medals, a military cap, a Luftwaffe badge and a black tie with the word 'Berlin' inscribed on it.

Faced with such damning evidence, Stephen Held spun a fantastic yarn. He told the police that a visitor named Heinrich Brandy had arrived at his house and asked to be put up for a short time. He had agreed to take in the mysterious Mr Brandy as a lodger. He said he did not know where the stranger was because he seemed to have disappeared. He denied any knowledge of the contents of Mr Brandy's room.

The evidence given at the trial of Stephen Held made it quite clear to the Irish Government that a German spy had arrived in Ireland. Held was sentenced to five years in gaol. The matter also aroused the intense interest of the German Ambassador in Dublin, Eduard Hempel. He was annoyed that he knew nothing of the arrival of a spy called Brandy. He contacted Berlin for an explanation and was told that Brandy was under instructions to make personal contacts in Ireland but not to undertake activities directed against the Irish Government. It was only much later that Hempel learned that Brandy's real name was Goertz. Hempel was called to the Department of External Affairs and he tried to convince the Assistant Secretary, Frederick

Dr Herman Goertz.

Boland, that Germany's respect for Irish neutrality was undiminished.

In Berlin, Major-General von Lahousen wrote in his diary that Operation Mainau had ended in failure. Proposals for the parachuting of further agents into Ireland were to be abandoned. Von Lahousen wrote that he did not know what had happened to Goertz.

After fleeing from Held's house in Templeogue, Goertz headed for Laragh Castle, only to discover that Iseult Stuart had been arrested. But a friend of Iseult Stuart, Helena Moloney, a leading member of the Women Workers' Union, was in the house when Goertz called and she arranged a number of safe houses where he could stay in Dublin. Goertz was, by this point, entirely fed up with the IRA and he decided that he would make his own arrangements, with Helena Moloney's assistance, to stay with those people whom he felt he could trust.

For the next nineteen months, until his arrest in November 1941, Goertz was sheltered and protected by a number of elderly ladies who could best be described as die-hard republicans. Goertz spent a number of days of each week at Miss Coffey's house at Charlemont Avenue, Dún Laoghaire (where the neighbours were told that he was a commercial traveller named Mr Robinson) and in a house in Dalkey, which was rented for him by Miss Maisie O'Mahony (daughter of the Dáil deputy, Seán O'Mahony). Miss O'Mahony acted as Goertz's chauffeur and secretary. He was supported financially by Mrs Caitlín Brugha, widow of Cathal Brugha. She owned the large Dublin firm Kingston Shirts. Later, Goertz stayed with Misses Mary and Bridie Farrell at their house in Glenageary.

For a time, a transmitter was installed at the house rented for Goertz in Dalkey. The radio operator was Anthony Deery and he transmitted Goertz's messages to Berlin. Various people, some allegedly Dáil deputies, met Goertz during the autumn and winter of 1940. One certain visitor was Major-General Hugo MacNeill, who commanded the second division of the Irish Army. Unknown to his army colleagues, MacNeill put forward a plan of action in case Britain should invade Ireland. MacNeill proposed that the Irish Government would seek German assistance, would offer Germany the use of Irish airfields and ports, and would make captured weapons available to Germany. If the Irish Government had discovered MacNeill's unauthorised dealings, he would surely have been court-marshalled. When the German Ambassador, Hempel, was apprised of these proposals, he judged wisely that de Valera would be unlikely to agree to them. Hempel feared that

Goertz was competing with him for control of German policy in Ireland. He dared not meet Goertz in case the Irish Government should find out, yet he knew that the threat of a British invasion was real and that the Irish Army needed support.

It was Goertz who took the initiative and suggested a meeting with Hempel. The Ambassador decided on the novel plan to host a party at the German Embassy, 58 Northumberland Road, to which Goertz would be invited and where he would be inconspicuous amid the stream of visitors. At intervals during the party, Hempel left his guests to have short conversations with Goertz. These took place in the study room of the embassy. Hempel was impressed by the agent's courtesy and intelligence. He was delighted when Goertz said that he wanted to return to Berlin to report fully on the Irish situation. Goertz had become too hot for Hempel to handle and the intrigues with Major-General MacNeill presented a serious threat to Irish neutrality. Hempel believed that the presence of a German spy in Ireland would be used as propaganda to force de Valera to enter the war against Germany.

Attempts were made in February and September 1941 to bring Goertz to the French coast by boat but they failed due to bad weather. In late autumn 1941, nearly all of Goertz's helpers were arrested, among them Jim O'Donovan, who had maintained regular contact with the German agent. The Irish police, with the help of the Intelligence Service, had discovered the addresses of most of the IRA's safe houses. Goertz knew that the net was closing in on him. He determined to go to France to report his belief that the Irish Army would support Germany if Britain attempted to seize Irish ports. But Goertz was too late. On 27 November 1941, while hiding in the house of P.J. Claffey at 1 Blackheath Park, Clontarf, the home of a Dublin girl with whom Goertz had developed a relationship, the police raided and found the German agent in the living room. There were suggestions of IRA treachery. Equally, there were suggestions that the Irish police had been tracking him for some time and had finally decided to arrest him. It was alleged that de Valera did not want Goertz to be arrested in case the war went in Germany's favour, meaning the police would have bungled by arresting him. Whichever the case, Goertz was soon in prison awaiting transfer to an internment camp. What is certain is that the Irish Intelligence Service had broken Goertz's radio code and had intercepted his messages to Berlin. Dr Richard Hayes, Director of the National Library and a cryptologist with the Intelligence Service, was credited with breaking Goertz's code. Colonel Éamon de Buitléir claimed that, in reality, he broke the code and not his boss, Dr Hayes. It is indeed probable that the police could have captured Goertz much earlier had they wished to do so.

A week after Goertz's arrest, the United States of America declared war against Japan following the Japanese attack on the naval base at Pearl Harbour. On 11 December, Germany and Italy declared war on the USA. Churchill asked de Valera to join the effort to destroy Germany, now that the USA had entered the fray. De Valera refused. On 26 January 1942, American troops arrived in Northern Ireland. Germany reacted to the developments in Ireland by preparing a Special Service

Troop which would be parachuted into Ireland to incite opposition in the event of an American–British decision to invade the country. As it happened, the plans proved unnecessary because Ireland was not invaded.

Goertz was questioned rigorously in Arbour Hill Military Prison, Dublin, but he refused to say anything. He was treated well, and in autumn 1942 he was transferred to Athlone Internment Camp. His cell there was fitted with carpet and bookshelves. There was a common room, a dining room, a yard and a small garden. Goertz was allowed to listen to Irish radio and to read Irish newspapers. Despite these good conditions, Goertz found prison life difficult and he determined to escape. He made elaborate plans and succeeded in conveying pleas for assistance to the German Ambassador, Hempel. But the Ambassador could do nothing, so Goertz's plans fell apart. As a lawyer, Goertz wanted to be put on trial. He could not understand why he was being interned without charge. He decided to go on hunger strike. It lasted three weeks, until other prisoners persuaded him that the Irish Secret Service would be delighted if he saved them the bother of deciding what to do with him by dying on hunger strike.

Goertz resigned himself to prison routine. He wrote two plays in German and made copious entries in his diary. He translated stories by W.B. Yeats into German. In one essay, Goertz wrote of his failed mission to Ireland, 'I often curse fate that I found friends here, friends who showed me the genius of the country. I fell in love with Ireland: the more upright a lover is, the more he suffers if his love is unrequited.'

Following Germany's surrender in May 1945, Colonel Éamon de Buitléir made an agreement with Goertz that he would not be deported with other internees if he made full statements about his activities in Ireland. Goertz claimed consistently that it was never his intention, nor that of his country, to violate Irish neutrality. In Germany, however, Major-General von Lahousen admitted at the Nuremburg War Trials that plans had been made to land German troops in Ireland. When Goertz heard about von Lahousen's admission, he determined not to be sent back to Germany for fear that he would be sentenced to death. Goertz was convinced that his actions had been honourable at all times.

On 10 September 1946, the Minister for Justice, Gerard Boland, announced that all German spies in Ireland would be offered political asylum. Boland's deliberate snub to Britain was an optimistic sign for Goertz. He began to settle down to Irish life and, once again, was given lodgings by the Farrell sisters in Glenageary. In February 1947, he got a job as Secretary of the Save the German Children Fund, an Irish relief organisation established to assist German children. Goertz sold small stools and other furniture to raise money for the organisation.

The Minister for Justice's decision to offer asylum to German spies was opposed by the Department of External Affairs. De Valera was persuaded that it was unwise to provoke British opposition further and he decided to reverse the decision. On 12 April 1941, police detectives arrested the former internees, including Goertz. From Mountjoy Gaol, Goertz sent a letter to de Valera pleading for asylum. He said that the Department of Justice had assured him that he would not be deported. While most other German spies were duly deported, Goertz was given parole to wind up his personal affairs in Ireland. This made Goertz highly agitated, and he sought the help of anyone he could to prevent his deportation. He was invited to dine with Hempel at his residence in Monkstown. Frederick Boland was also present at the dinner. Goertz was asked if he would consider working for the Americans. He asked for time to consider the proposal. Following the meal, Goertz met another ex-internee Luftwaffe officer, George Fleischmann, at the Royal Marine Hotel, Dún Laoghaire, and throughout the night, they discussed Hempel and Boland's proposition. Fleischmann encouraged Goertz to accept the offer, but Goertz was convinced that he was being double-crossed and that he would be deported. He went to the west of Ireland for a few days to calm his nerves. When he returned to Dublin, he learned that he had been requested to report on Friday, 23 May 1947, to the Aliens' Registration Office at Dublin Castle in order to have his parole extended. He had also been invited to lunch with Hempel on that day. Goertz never arrived at the Ambassador's house. He was convinced that his deportation was imminent, and soon after he arrived at the Aliens' Office, he swallowed the contents of his phial of potassium cyanide. He was rushed to Mercer's Hospital by ambulance but was dead on arrival.

Due to bureaucratic bungling, Hempel and Boland's plan that Goertz should work for the Americans was not relayed to the Intelligence Service. When Goertz arrived at the Aliens' Office, a Special Branch man, Detective Sergeant McConnell, told Goertz that a plane was waiting to fly him back to Germany. Goertz panicked and resolved to commit suicide. It is probable that he had planned to do so, because in the previous three months he had carved his own tombstone and sculpted a relief on it which was richly symbolic – a sword sheathed in barbed wire.

Attempts were made to give Goertz a military funeral but the Irish Government refused. Instead, Goertz's remains, clothed in Fleischmann's great coat, were laid to rest at Deansgrange Cemetery on Monday, 26 May 1947. The coffin was draped in a swastika flag. Among those in attendance were Jim O'Donovan, Anthony Deery and Misses Mary and Bridie Farrell, who proudly wore Goertz's medals. The German Ambassador, Hempel, was advised by the Irish Government that it would be inappropriate for him to attend the funeral. The Deansgrange Cemetery records state that Goertz was 'fifty-six, Protestant, married' and gave his address as '7 Spencer Villas, Glenageary', the home of the Farrell sisters.

On 13 June 1947, an inquest on Goertz's death was held by the Dublin City Coroner, Dr McErlean. The Senior Counsel acting for Goertz, John A. Costello (who, two years later, became Taoiseach in the first inter-party government), asked the jury 'to do nothing that would in any way besmirch this man's memory. He was ... a German soldier doing what he considered to be his duty.' The jury brought in a verdict of death due to cardiac failure following the swallowing of poison and made no further comment.

In a letter to *The Irish Times*, Donal O'Sullivan (who lived at Cairn Hill, Foxrock, and was Clerk of the Senate of the Irish Free State) wrote, 'I would urge on humanitarian grounds ... that, for the future, any peaceable, self-supporting German who is already in Ireland and wishes to remain here should be allowed to do so. There is already enough misery in the world without adding to it.' Thankfully, Dr O'Sullivan's advice has been heeded.

The final twist in the tale of Dr Hermann Goertz occurred in 1974, when his mortal remains were exhumed, under cover of night, by some German ex-army officers. They were transferred from Deansgrange Cemetery to the German War Cemetery at Glencree, County Wicklow. A bizarre end to a strange story.

References and Further Reading

Newspapers

'Hermann Goertz Takes His Life', *Evening Herald*, 23 May 1947.

'Goertz Funeral', *The Irish Times,* 26 May 1947.

'Poison Verdict on German Parachutist', *Irish Press*, 14 June 1947.

Hermann Goertz, 'Mission to Ireland', *The Irish Times*, 25, 27, 29 August and 1, 3, 5, 8, 10 September 1947. These eight articles provide Goertz's own useful but fanciful account of his mission to Ireland.

Kees Van Hoek, 'Secret Agents in Ireland', *Sunday Chronicle*, 9 & 16 May 1954.

M. O'Halloran, 'German Master Spy's Suicide in Dublin', *Sunday Press*, 27 June 1957.

Charles Wighton & Gunter Peis, 'Goertz's Mission Fails', *The Irish Times*, 4 June 1958.

Books

Bowyer Bell, J., *The Secret Army* (London, 1970).

Carroll, Joseph T., *Ireland in the War Years 1939-1945* (Newton Abbot, 1975).

Duggan, John P., *Neutral Ireland and the Third Reich* (Dublin, 1985).

Fisk, Robert, *In Time of War* (London, 1983).

Garter, Carolle, *The Shamrock and the Swastika* (London, 1977).

Stephan, Enno, *Spies in Ireland* (London, 1963).

4

William Dargan of Mount Anville: Great Railway Builder and Patriot

by Brian Mac Aongusa (2010)

It is difficult in a short paper to do justice to the achievements of William Dargan – the great nineteenth-century builder of railways, canals and harbours, as well as the instigator of many philanthropic projects throughout the island of Ireland. He was a pioneering developer driven by an ethic of hard work, duty and decency. Moreover, for over fifteen years of his life he lived in The Dargan Villa near Goatstown, better known today as Mount Anville Sacred Heart Secondary School for Girls. It was there, in 1853, that Queen Victoria, Prince Albert and the young English princes paid a most unusual visit to a commoner in his own home and offered to make him a baronet. However, William Dargan declined to accept the honour.

In 1864, this extraordinary man, while still alive, had the distinctive honour of having a statue of himself unveiled by the Lord Lieutenant at Merrion Square, Dublin. It was to mark the public's gratitude to him for instilling national self-confidence in the aftermath of the Great

Famine. It was also in recognition of his single-handed funding of the Great Exhibition of Art & Industry in 1853, on the lawn of Leinster House, Dublin, which led directly to the founding of the National Gallery of Ireland. William Dargan was a modest man who worked extremely hard throughout his life to develop the resources of his country for his own people. By 1863, he had built over 1,000 miles of railway in Ireland and had become known as the 'Founder of Irish Railways'.

William Dargan, the great railway builder and patriot.

Early Life and Work

Dargan was born near Carlow town on 28 February 1799, the eldest in a large family working as tenant-farmers on the estate of the Earl of Portarlington. It is believed he went to a local hedge school in Graiguecullen near Carlow, where he excelled in mathematics and accounting. Afterwards, he worked on his father's 101-acre farm before starting in a surveyor's office in Carlow. With the help of some influential patrons, especially John Alexander, a prominent miller in County Carlow, and Sir Henry Parnell, MP for Queen's County who then chaired the Parliamentary Commission for Improving the London–Holyhead Road, William Dargan secured a position with the renowned Scottish engineer of that project, Thomas Telford, at the Holyhead end of the road.

It was there, from 1819 to 1824, that he learned many of his building skills. At first he was an inspector of works, and then resident engineer of the 1,300-yard embankment carrying the road – and later the railway – across the Stanley Sands sea inlet to Holy Island. That was William Dargan's first engineering project. Thomas Telford was so impressed with Dargan's work that he asked him to survey and to supervise construction at the Irish end of the project, which was a new road with a seaward stone wall from Raheny to Sutton serving the then mail-packet station at Howth. When completed, this new road was described by Henry Parnell as 'a model for other roads in the vicinity of Dublin' and it earned the young William Dargan a premium of £300 from the Treasury in London. This significant sum provided the basic capital for his future business as a major public works contractor.

During the 1820s, Dargan secured contracts for other works in the Dublin region, including the North Circular Road and the Malahide turnpike, as well as the Carlow and Dunleer turnpikes. In 1824, he became superintendent of the Barrow Navigation. He undertook many other construction works, including embankment works on the River Shannon at Limerick, the excavation of a large cut through the centre of Banbridge, County Down, to make it easier for mail coaches to reach the top of the town, and the construction of the Kilbeggan branch of the Grand Canal. In the 1820s, William Dargan met his Welsh wife Jane in the English Midlands, but details of their marriage are not known and the couple had no children.

Dublin and Kingstown Railway

In 1831, William Dargan achieved his first big breakthrough, when, beating six other competitors, he won the prestigious contract to build Ireland's first railway from Dublin to Kingstown, now Dún Laoghaire. The engineer was another famous Telford pupil, Charles Vignoles.

Dargan began work in April 1833, when his men began 'to cut down the cliffs at Salthill'. As was his practice, he made haste to get work going at a number of places along the line, but not without initial difficulties with landowners and labourers. Two landowners at Blackrock – Baron Cloncurry of Maretimo and the Revd Sir Harcourt Lees of Blackrock House – declared that they could not bear to have their estates desecrated by a railway. Lengthy negotiations were necessary to persuade them to allow the building of the line. Final agreement was only secured with an undertaking that the Dublin and Kingstown Railway would construct a tunnel, towers, piers, bridges and bathing places in the best Italian style and of finely worked granite along the seaward extremity of their lands. This gave Dargan a golden opportunity to demonstrate his construction skills.

Dargan was essentially a builder, not an assembler of other men's products. The material of bridges, walls, embankments and even the railway sleepers had to be fashioned by his own craftsmen. He had to provide a very large workforce and a great number of wheelbarrows, picks and shovels so that many labourers might work together on the embankments. Stonecutters were a big proportion of his employees. Granite from Dalkey quarries was brought down by the harbour tramway to Kingstown and then transported in small boats to wherever needed. A piece of good fortune was the discovery of a bed of fine granite at Seapoint.

William Dargan's intentions in relation to work practice initially caused difficulties and gave rise to a couple of short-lived strikes. Dargan paid his workers, each according to his ability, 10s, 9s or 8s a week. This scale did not satisfy all the men, some of whom talked their companions into a work stoppage, as reported by the *Dublin Evening Post* of 4 June 1833:

> On Saturday the infatuated workmen engaged in the Rail-road at Seapoint objected to work unless paid ten shillings per week instead of nine ... One man called together

several of the workmen and, whistling 'Patrick's Day' and 'Boyne Water', led them through masses of labourers on the shore, encouraging them not to work unless they received higher salaries.

For a few days, no work was done and some rioting ensued. The police were called and the leaders were arrested. Their followers lost a week's earnings, causing the strike to lose much of its popularity. William Dargan then announced he would pay by results and the men who took his offer found it to their advantage. This new policy encouraged the strong and the willing, and differed from the custom of paying a flat rate for the week. The strike movement did not gain further support. In fact, most men appreciated the fact that Dargan paid higher wages to unskilled labourers than had been customary in Ireland. Money was now circulating in the district; morale improved and there was a marked decline in petty crime. The only local objections emerged during the summer months when some scandalised Monkstown residents complained that Mr Dargan's workers were bathing during their lunch hour 'in an indelicate state'.

The railway to Kingstown was built on a series of embankments between Merrion and Dún Laoghaire. The construction of these sea embankments, laid on the strand, required a very large workforce. By July 1833, Dargan had 1,500 men working, and by September that figure had risen to 1,800. By October, work at the Dublin end was going on by day and night, but progress was slowed by what was described as 'the extreme inclemency of the weather'. Yet in spite of a flood in the River Dodder wrecking the new railway bridge at

Ballsbridge and requiring a replacement to be built in October 1834, the Dublin and Kingstown Railway was finally opened to public traffic on 17 December 1834.

The successful completion of Ireland's first railway enormously enhanced William Dargan's reputation and placed him in the front rank of Irish public works contractors. The Dublin and Kingstown Railway was described by its directors as 'a triumph of engineering and constructive ability'. Fine examples of Dargan's work on the line have survived to this day in the embankments and sea walls from Merrion to Salthill. There is also the magnificent outer granite wall of the former Dublin and Kingstown Railway terminus opposite the present-day Stena Line terminal building in Dún Laoghaire.

Dargan Moves to Belfast

The construction of Ireland's second railway – the Ulster railway from Belfast to Lisburn – had progressed more slowly, reaching Lisburn five years later in 1839.

The Dublin and Kingstown Railway, showing the first, second, third and fourth class carriages drawn by the locomotive Hibernia

The Dublin and Kingstown Railway, Ireland's first.

Requiring more rapid progress, the directors of the Ulster Railway contracted Dargan to extend their line to Portadown and later to Armagh. William Dargan then based himself in Belfast, and over the next decade worked on a variety of projects in the north of Ireland. These included the construction of the Ulster Canal to connect Lough Erne with Lough Neagh, and the operation of passenger and goods boats between Newry, Enniskillen, Belfast and all points on Loughs Neagh and Erne and attached navigations. Other projects in the North included the reclamation of extensive mudflats along the southern shore of Lough Foyle, the building of two artificial lakes for mill owners in County Down, and the creation of a deep shipping channel and shipping berths at the mouth of the River Lagan in Belfast. The last of these was achieved by excavating considerable quantities of mud, which were then deposited on the County Down side of the Lagan, which became known as Dargan's Island. When Queen Victoria visited Belfast in 1849 it was renamed Queen's Island and developed as a public park. Later on, it became the famous Harland & Wolff shipyards. Modern Belfast has recently honoured Dargan by naming the new cross-city viaduct over the River Lagan the William Dargan Bridge.

Dargan in Demand

During the 'railway mania' that developed in the 1840s, Dargan was very much in demand, as newly established companies planned to build railways to other parts of Ireland. At that time, it was the practice for such companies to divide a contract for the first segment of their planned line among different contractors so as to identify the best among them. Invariably, the section given to William Dargan proved to be the best constructed, and companies tended to ask him to take charge of building the remainder of the line without engaging other contractors. In this way, he became known as the great builder of railways in Ireland. By 1853, he had constructed over 600 miles of railway under contracts totalling some £2,000,000, had other contracts for a further 200 miles, and employed a workforce of more than 50,000 men. It has been estimated that Dargan paid out some £4,000,000 in wages to his workers between 1845 and 1850.

It is quite remarkable that Dargan succeeded in carrying out so many simultaneous contracts in various parts of the country at a time when travel and communication was only possible on horseback, in horse-drawn vehicles or by boat. He had to carefully choose competent and trustworthy people to manage many contracts during lengthy periods of his absence. Clearly, William Dargan must have been an excellent judge of men on whose integrity and skill he could rely, because in executing major construction contracts he made few, if any, mistakes. It is also significant that many of those whom he trained and trusted with senior responsibility during his absences subsequently became eminent railway builders in their own right later in the nineteenth century.

Dargan's construction works have enhanced our railway system throughout Ireland and a cursory glance of some examples will help to illustrate his achievements.

As well as the Dublin and Kingstown Railway, the magnificent 'Nine Arches' granite viaduct at Milltown is still used to this day by Luas. The first intended terminus of the Dublin, Dundrum and Rathfarnham Railway, beside the modern Luas stop at Dundrum, also built by William Dargan, still survives. Many other fine examples of works constructed by him may still be seen all over Ireland, north and south, east and west. The highest and longest railway viaduct in Ireland, built on a curving incline of 1:130 and consisting of eighteen arches of local granodiorite stone, rises 137 feet above the Camlough River near Newry, making it the tallest railway bridge in Ireland. The original viaduct built by Dargan is still in use today.

The Great Famine

Many of William Dargan's achievements must be viewed against the background of the misery and poverty that resulted from the greatest social disaster to have hit Ireland in recent times, namely the Great Famine, which lasted from 1845 to 1850. Most of the railway projects had been floated with much optimism in pre-Famine times, but after the black years of 1847/48 when up to 1 million people died of hunger, the financial state of many railway companies approached near ruin. In spite of this, Dargan succeeded in keeping a surprising number of works going through a system of credit, under which he agreed to accept bonds or shares in the railway companies instead of cash payments. Many schemes and workers' jobs at that time were saved from extinction by the special credit arrangements agreed to and put in place by William Dargan.

In these modern times, it seems strange that an astute man of Dargan's standing should not have insisted on being paid properly for his work. The reason, I believe, he was prepared to risk so much of his fortune in supporting the building of railways during very depressed times, was his determination that never again would his country have to experience the horrors he had seen during those Famine years. Food, as is well known, was sent to Ireland from charities abroad, but what is less well known is that most of it lay at the ports because of the lack of transport to carry it to those dying of hunger. Thanks to his determination to continue to finance the building of railways throughout the Famine period and its aftermath, many an Irish family survived to bless the great William Dargan, who was fondly known in the west of Ireland as 'An Fear Traenach' (The Railway Man). It is recorded that, when recruiting workers for his schemes in those terrible years, Dargan would pay those selected a full week's wages in advance and tell them he did not expect any work from them until they had some nourishment and got their strength back.

Another example of Dargan's great humanity may be found in a report of his action following the formal ceremony of turning the first sod of the Waterford and Limerick Railway by the Earl of Clare in a field near Boher, County Limerick, on 15 October 1846:

Dargan distributed a large sum of money to the several country people present and £5 to James McCormack, tenant of the field, so that he might entertain his neighbours.

The dignitaries then returned to Limerick for a splendid
dinner in Cruise's Hotel, the party numbering forty.

This was probably why the press of the day, when
writing about William Dargan, frequently referred to
him as 'The Man with his Hand in his Pocket'. But
when Dargan himself referred to such instances or to
his generous treatment of his workers, he was quoted by
a contemporary railway engineer, William Le Fanu as
frequently saying, 'A spoonful of honey will catch more
flies than a gallon of vinegar.'

A fascinating insight to the work ethic of William
Dargan may be gleaned from his approach to extending
the Midland and Great Western Railway mainline from
Mullingar to Galway between 1849 and 1851. The
company had been successful in June 1849 in obtaining a
government loan of £500,000 for the Galway extension,
on the grounds that it would save the people of the
western counties from starvation by creating employment
on the railway. The directors lost no time in entering into
a contract with Dargan, and, with great dedication, he
tackled his challenging task. By mid-August he had some
600 men employed on the works and, in spite of some
initial local protests when he recruited paupers from the
workhouse in Mullingar, his workforce had reached 6,000
by the following April and topped 9,000 by September
1850. The entire line was completed by mid-July 1851,
five months in advance of the time specified in the
Galway Extension Act. To achieve this remarkable goal,
Dargan involved himself totally in his work, by living,
sleeping and operating on site from a mobile office that
was propelled along the new railway as it was extending

westwards. This office, which became known as 'The Dargan Saloon', may still be seen preserved in the Ulster Folk & Transport Museum at Cultra, County Down.

Philanthropic Work

By the early 1850s, when William Dargan had begun to amass a substantial fortune from his numerous contracts, his one ambition was to use it to develop the resources of his own country. As one example, Dargan had noted in the north of Ireland that flax was grown as a very profitable crop and he planned to extend its benefits to farmers in the south of Ireland. He bought a 2,000 acre farm near Rathcormac in County Cork, where he experimented in flax cultivation and built a number of flax mills. He offered to supply flax seed to all farmers in the locality at his own expense and to purchase their crops from them at the current Belfast prices. However, very few Cork farmers accepted his offer. When asked what punitive action he would take in the light of this failed experiment, Dargan was reported to have replied, 'Never show your teeth unless you can bite.'

He enjoyed a greater measure of success with a philanthropic project at Chapelizod near Dublin. William Dargan took over an old-established flax-thread mill and spent large sums on renovations and extensions. For years he operated this plant, known as the Dargan & Haughton Mills, and employed up to 900 people, producing a very good product, which won an award for quality at a Paris exhibition in 1855. William Dargan was always regarded at the mills as a good employer, and in July 1860 he took 700 employees by a sixteen-coach special train from Harcourt Street station in Dublin to Bray, where they dined and danced at his expense before returning to Dublin by train in the evening.

The following extract from an article describing the outing to Bray in *Saunder's Newsletter* of 30 July 1860 is of interest:

> Saturday was a gala day to the numerous persons – men, women, boys and girls – amounting in all to upwards of 700 employed in Mr Dargan's extensive linen, flax and thread mills at Chapelizod, County Dublin. At an early hour they were all marshalled in holiday attire and walked in procession, headed by the private band of the factory, under the able direction of Mr Bell ... An auxiliary band of drums and fifes took up the inspiring strain to cheer the joyful party on their march to Harcourt Street Terminus; a special train was in waiting, and at a quarter before ten o'clock, sixteen carriages were filled with the happy crowd, anxious to see sights they never before saw, and many never expected to see ... The appearance of the females was in the highest degree creditable. They were neat and tidy in dress, most becoming and orderly in their behaviour ... At half-past seven (in the evening) this gratified crowd left by special train in the same order in which they arrived, blessing the name of their good employer, William Dargan, who afforded them such a day's pleasure unalloyed in every sense, except by the unfortunate state of the weather.

Dargan became involved in many other philanthropic projects aimed at encouraging development in the post-Famine period. Among his other projects were a distillery at Belturbet, County Cavan, a sugar-beet plant at Mountmellick, County Laois, and the substantial reclamation of sloblands near Wexford town. At various places in Ireland, including Raheny near Dublin, he bought areas of farmland, grew sugar-beet and applied modern methods and large capital sums to their improvement. At agricultural shows in Ireland and in England he won many prizes for growing sugar beet and many varieties of vegetables. He bought a beautiful residence, known as The Dargan Villa at Mount Anville, near Dundrum, County Dublin, added a campanile viewing tower to it, and reared fine breeds of sheep and cattle in the surrounding grounds. The flowers from his gardens and greenhouses at Mount Anville were famous at exhibitions around Dublin.

Mount Anville, the home of William Dargan.

The Great Exhibition of Art & Industry, 1853

William Dargan was an able and constant advocate of Ireland and Irish enterprise, and was untiring in his efforts to develop his native land. After the successful Crystal Palace Exhibition in London in 1851, Dargan proposed and single-handedly financed the Great Exhibition of Art & Industry in Dublin from May to October 1853. His objective was to showcase the best of Irish art and industry to help counter the negative image of the country in the wake of the Famine. He constructed an extensive iron and glass building on the RDS-owned Leinster Lawn, facing Merrion Square, to house the exhibition, which was more a celebration of art than a display of Irish industry or engineering. Yet it proved a triumph for William Dargan as an important expression of national self-confidence. No fewer than 1.1 million visitors from Ireland and abroad came to Dublin for the exhibition, and in August 1853, Queen Victoria, Prince Albert and the two young English princes travelled to Dublin and honoured the exhibition with a royal visit.

Despite its great success, Dargan's expenditure of over £100,000 in making the exhibition possible was not fully recouped, and he lost about £20,000 on the venture, which was a setback, even for such a wealthy man. But such was the impact and perceived success of the great event, which displayed over a thousand works of fine art included at the insistence of William Dargan himself, that a testimonial subscription was formed in July 1853 to establish a permanent public art collection as a fitting monument to Dargan's vision and munificence. This led to the founding of the National

Gallery of Ireland in 1854 on the exhibition site and to the unveiling, ten years later by the Lord Lieutenant, of a fine bronze statue of Dargan by Thomas Farrell, which still stands today outside the National Gallery.

Visit of Queen Victoria

In those times, it was rare for a monarch to visit a commoner in his home, but Queen Victoria, immediately after her arrival in Ireland in August 1853, journeyed from Kingstown to the home of William Dargan and his wife Jane at Mount Anville near Dundrum. The

A train at Foxrock Station.

royal party were brought up to the campanile tower to get a 360-degree view, which was described by them as being 'unequalled in Ireland'. The *Illustrated London News* of 10 September 1853 included a full feature article entitled 'The Dargan Villa, Mount Anville – Visit of Her Majesty'. It praises the villa, its location, interior layout and grounds in fulsome terms, 'Her Majesty, who warmly expressed her surprise and delight, seemed riveted to views to the north; and the whole royal party, indeed, expressed a similar feeling.'

The Queen's diary of the visit records that she wished to bestow on Dargan a baronetcy in recognition of his considerable achievements, but he politely declined the honour without any reason being recorded. William Dargan always maintained that he only worked for the betterment of his own country, but his family believed that he refused Queen Victoria's offer because of the way he saw the Irish people in his youth being mistreated in Carlow.

The Development of Bray

With the revival of hope in Ireland after 1853, William Dargan built the large No.1 Graving Dock at Dublin Port to accommodate the Holyhead paddle steamers and returned to railway construction, particularly the Dublin and Wicklow Railway, which reached Bray in 1854 and was completed to Wicklow in 1855. Some 500 men were employed on this last section, which involved difficult tunnelling through very hard Precambrian rock under Bray Head. In those depressed post-Famine years, Dargan once again agreed to accept payment in bonds, which later were exchanged for shares in the railway company. His very large holding led to his selection as a director of the Dublin and Wicklow Railway in 1856, and later, in 1864, he was elected chairman of the company. By this time, William Dargan had been involved in building over 1,000 miles of railway in Ireland.

It was now Dargan's ambition to develop a seaside resort at Bray, which had only been a small fishing village on the arrival of the railway. Dargan devoted considerable energy to having the projected resort modelled on Brighton in south-east England in order to provide a pleasant watering place for the people of Dublin within easy reach of the city by train.

He laid out a seafront esplanade, built fashionable Turkish baths and a substantial terrace of houses, developed wide roads, a fair green, a market, and helped to install gas lights in the new town. He was also a major investor in the modern, 130-bedroom International Hotel near the railway station.

Because of his substantial investment in Bray, William Dargan was elected one of its Town Commissioners in 1860. He was hailed as 'The Friend of Ireland' and was credited with the transformation of the one-street town into a developed seaside resort that has since attracted thousands of visitors each year.

Tragedy Strikes

On 1 May 1865, tragedy struck William Dargan. While riding along the Stillorgan Road, a woman shaking out a white sheet from a house window caused his horse, to shy, throwing him heavily on the ground. He was concussed and badly injured, and he never fully recovered. A few months later, Dargan was obliged, despite his wife's strong objections, to sell Mount Anville to an order of nuns that still operates a girls' secondary school there. Subsequently, he had a further fall, and his business interests suffered due to his inability to devote his full attention to them. In 1866, the financial crisis in Britain and the collapse of bankers Overend & Gurney, caused railway shares to plummet and Dargan appointed trustees to run his business. This move alarmed his creditors and caused a further decline in his fortunes. His health deteriorated due to a malignant liver disease and he made his will in January 1867. Not long afterwards, on 7 February 1867, he died in his Dublin townhouse at 2 Fitzwilliam Square aged sixty-eight years.

Tributes

Lengthy tributes to William Dargan, 'The Workman's Friend', appeared in the press both in Ireland and in England, and his funeral on 11 February was the largest seen in Dublin since that of Daniel O'Connell some twenty years earlier. The cortège, which travelled from his residence at 2 Fitzwilliam Square to Glasnevin Cemetery, was led by some 700 railway workers from various companies with whom Dargan was associated. The hearse, drawn by four horses, was followed by three mourning coaches, the Lord Mayor's State Chariot and a long line of over 250 carriages carrying a wide range of people from many parts of the country. Dargan was laid to rest in a vault among the great in the O'Connell Circle at Glasnevin Cemetery. His elegant tomb is almost certainly the work of the architect John Skipton Mulvany, who had designed Broadstone, Blackrock and Kingstown railway stations.

This remarkable funeral was clearly a powerful public recognition of William Dargan's endeavours to raise the status of his country and give hope to its people in deeply distressing times. As providence had denied him the gift of children, he seemed to have adopted Ireland as his child and used all the benefits of his education and experience to try to raise the standard of Irish life and business. This is the only feasible explanation for his investment of huge sums of money in so many unprofitable enterprises. It was indeed fitting that in 2004, when the new Luas Green Line was opened, the magnificent cable-stayed bridge at Dundrum was formally named the William J. Dargan Bridge, in the presence of a kinsman, Fr Daniel Dargan SJ, who passed away in 2006.

Perhaps the most revealing insight to the character of the man may be found in a book of reminiscences, *Seventy Years of Irish Life*, by a contemporary railway engineer, William Le Fanu, who describes his business dealings with William Dargan as follows:

> I have settled as engineer for different companies many of his accounts, involving many hundreds of thousand pounds. His thorough honesty, his willingness to yield a disputed point and his wonderful rapidity of decision, rendered it

a pleasure, instead of a trouble as it generally is, to settle these accounts. Indeed in my life I have never met a man more quick in intelligence, more clear-sighted and more thoroughly honourable.

The modern suspension bridge named after William Dargan at Dundrum.

Conclusion

William Dargan was a man removed from the turmoil of party politics, but nevertheless was an inspiration to his countrymen. The news that he had consented to taking shares in a downcast company was the signal for an instant revival of hope, which, in almost all cases, proved to be justified. He was variously referred to in his own lifetime as 'The Man with his Hand in his Pocket', 'An Fear Traenach', 'The Workman's Friend' and 'The Friend of Ireland'. These extraordinary public endorsements, together with his undoubted skill, integrity, humanity and enormous capacity for hard work on behalf of his own people, made William Dargan, in my view, a practical and truly outstanding patriot in nineteenth-century Ireland.

References and Further Reading

Cassells, Brian, *The Ulster Canal* (Inland Waterways Association of Ireland, 2000).

Cox, R.C. & Gould, M.H., *Civil Engineering Heritage – Ireland* (London, 1998).

Crossland, B. & Moore, J.S., *The Lives of Great Engineers of Ulster, Vol. I* (Leicester, 2003).

Fayle, H. & Newham, A.T., *The Waterford & Tramore Railway* (David & Charles, 1972).

Fryer, C.E.J., *The Waterford & Limerick Railway* (The Oakwood Press, 2000).

Le Fanu, W.R., *Seventy Years of Irish Life* (Dublin, 1893).

Lowry, Mary, *The Story of Belfast: Chapter XX, Shipbuilding* (Library Ireland, 1913).

Mulligan, Fergus, *Bibliographical Dictionary of Civil Engineering Vol. 2* 1830-1890 (London, 2008).

Murray, K.A., *Ireland's First Railway* (Irish Railway Record Society, Dublin, 1981).

Murray, K.A. & McNeill, D.B., *The Great Southern & Western Railway* (Irish Railway Record Society, 1976).

Patterson, Edward M., *The Belfast & County Down Railway* (David & Charles, 1982).

Patterson, Edward M., *The Great Northern Railway (Ireland)* (The Oakwood Press, 2003).

Rynne, Colin, *Industrial Ireland, 1750-1930* (Cork, 2006).

Share, Bernard, *Irish Lives: Biographies of Fifty Famous Irish Men and Women* (Allen Figgis, Dublin, 1974).

Shepherd, Ernie, *The Midland Great Western Railway Company of Ireland* (Midland Publishing, 1994).

Shepherd, Ernie, *Waterford, Limerick and Western Railway* (Ian Allan Publishing, 2006).

Catalogue of 1853 *Exhibition, Memoir of William Dargan* (Irish Railway Record Society Library).

Journals of the Irish Railway Record Society, Volumes 2, 3, 11 and 13-19.

5

The Dundrum, Foxrock and Kingstown Junction Railway, 1865

by Liam Clare (2000)

The Context of the 1860s

Dublin, like other cities in the 1860s, was served by a number of inter-urban railway companies, each with a city terminal located at the edge of the inner city area nearest to the direction from which their trains arrived.

Thus, the Great Southern and Western Railway line from Cork, Limerick and the south-west terminated at Kingsbridge, now Heuston, on the south-western edge of the city centre; the Midland and Great Western Railway from Galway and Sligo terminated at the Broadstone, on the north-west edge; the Dublin and Drogheda Railway ran to Amiens Street; the Dublin and Kingstown line came from the south-east to Westland Row, and the Dublin and Wicklow line ended at Harcourt Street. A new radial line was being proposed to run from Trinity Street towards Rathfarnham and Brittas, and hopefully, in the future, towards Baltinglass. Stations were planned at South Circular

Road, Leinster Road, Rathgar Road, Rathfarnham, Templeogue, and Tallaght, among others, and it had the interesting name of the Dublin, Rathmines, Rathgar, Roundtown, Rathfarnham and Rathcoole Railway (DRRRR&RR).[1]

Rail transport was so far ahead of horse-drawn transport, with regard to capacity and speed, that an important public issue in Dublin and other urban areas was how to overcome the geographical inflexibility of the new form of transport and enable passengers and goods to move freely from place to place within the city.

Consequently, as in the case of other cities, moves were afoot in the mid-1860s to interconnect the

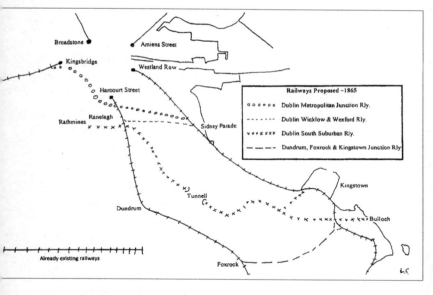

The railway proposals for Dublin, 1865, show how a number of interconnecting railway lines were planned. In the event, none of these were built, following the financial collapse of 1866.

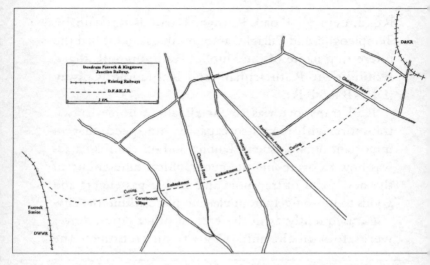

Route map for the Dundrum, Foxrock and Kingstown Junction Railway

isolated lines and to provide a central station. There was the proposed Dublin Trunk Connection Railway, linking Kingsbridge – via the Phoenix Park and the Royal Canal – with the Broadstone line, the Amiens Street line, the docks and – via a tunnel under the Liffey – to the Dublin and Kingstown Railway at a point near Serpentine Avenue.[2]

In 1863, there was one scheme which provoked huge opposition: the Dublin Metropolitan Railway, which was to run behind the buildings which fronted on to the South Quays from Kingsbridge eastwards to a central station at Fleet Street, with links to Westland Row and to other termini. One proposed feature, a bridge over Westmoreland Street, was particularly opposed on environmental grounds. The bill promoting the scheme in parliament was finally stopped in its tracks in the

House of Commons, after lobbying by the 'Dublin Six' – the six MPs from Dublin City. This proposal generated an antipathy among Dubliners to any city-centre connecting line, so the railway promoters looked towards the future interconnection of city railways by means of a southern suburban route.[3]

The procedure at the time for securing the necessary parliamentary approval for a railway scheme was to publish the proposals at the end of November in a particular year and to lodge the text of the bill, with plans, drawings and other documentation, for consideration by a committee of members of the House of Lords. These committees typically sat for a few weeks around the end of March, and heard the cases *for* the bill from the promoters, and *against* the proposals from existing commercial interests (particularly from existing railway companies), from local authorities, from landowners affected by the proposals, and from other interested parties. The committees tried to ensure that resources were not wasted on lines which duplicated existing services, and that lines which had been already approved would have a reasonable prospect of success. If, after hearing the evidence, the bill was approved in the Lords it was forwarded to the House of Commons, where another committee of MPs would hear any additional evidence presented, and if all went well, the approval of parliament would be secured around the end of July. Parliamentary approval did not, of course, mean that the scheme would ever be built; despite the precautions taken to weed out non-viable schemes, most schemes approved by parliament later perished on the rocks of inability to raise sufficient finance or other unforeseen obstacles.

The Railway-boom Proposals of 1864-5

In November 1863 alone, seven railway and tramway proposals for the Dublin area were announced – a figure exceeded by the eleven proposals submitted in November 1864 for consideration by parliament in 1865.[4]

These included four competing proposals on the south side – two inner suburban connecting links and two other links serving the outer suburbs (see map on p. 83). The first inner suburban link was a line between Kingsbridge and Harcourt Street, via the DRRRR&RR, continuing on to join up with the Westland Row to Kingstown line near Sydney Parade. The second part of this proposal was subsequently dropped. The second inner suburban link was the Dublin and Wicklow Railway Company's proposal to link the Harcourt Street and Westland Row lines via Ranelagh and Sydney Parade. The outer links – which are of more direct concern to us – were the Dublin South Suburban Railway, and the Dundrum, Foxrock and Kingstown Junction Railway.[5]

The last two proposals sought to link the middle-class areas of the coastal strip around Kingstown with the Rathmines and Rathgar Township, and to provide an additional route from Kingstown Harbour to the city and beyond.[6]

When the House of Lords committee met on 27 March 1865 and subsequent days, the Dublin and Wicklow Company were first called on to explain their proposal. During their presentation they stated in passing that there was a proposal for a third line to Bray. This was perhaps a mistake, or more likely a reference to a further future extension of the proposed Dublin South Suburban Railway, whose promoters were even at that stage planning to extend their proposed Rathmines to Bulloch line in the future with an extension to Killiney.[7]

The Rathmines to Bulloch proposal was next to be presented. The Dublin South Suburban Railway's line was to run from the DRRRR&RR at Leinster Road via Ranelagh, Milltown, Clonskeagh, Roebuck, Mount Merrion (where it would be carried in a tunnel under Mount Merrion Demesne) and then by Stillorgan, Carysfort, Kill, Monkstown, Kingstown, and Glenageary, to Bulloch near Dalkey. It would have a branch to the West Pier at Kingstown, which was to be approached through a tunnel. This proposed branch was soon dropped because of opposition from Lords Longford and de Vesci.[8]

Various people gave evidence to the committee, for and against the proposal, on the basis of whether such a service was needed, whether it duplicated other already approved lines, and whether it unnecessarily adversely affected property. The committee, having heard the evidence, deferred a decision on this scheme until the competing Dundrum, Foxrock and Kingstown Junction Railway was considered.[9]

The Dundrum, Foxrock and Kingstown Junction Proposal

This proposal was then presented to the committee. The railway would have used the existing Harcourt

Street Line from Dundrum to Foxrock, where it would deviate from the existing railway to run on a single track to a point just north of Glenageary station on the Kingstown to Dalkey track. At the time, the entire route crossed an undeveloped rural area.[10]

It would have left the existing railway line just to the north of Foxrock railway station, to swing south-eastward before crossing the present Westminster Road at what is now Primrose Cottage. In the submitted plans, a revised road network at the Foxrock village end of Torquay and Westminster Roads would have ensured that one simple level crossing would carry the trains across both roads (see map on p. 94). Having passed through – literally – Primrose Cottage, then the only residence on Westminster Road, the line would have headed eastwards in a cutting, across what is now Gordon Avenue, to a point just north of Cornelscourt Garage, where it would have crossed above a realigned main Bray Road east of Cornelscourt village, lowered sufficiently for the railway to cross above.[11]

After Cornelscourt (see map on p. 89), the line was to run along an embankment across the Clonkeen Valley, to a point between Pottery Road and Rochestown Avenue, where it again would have entered a cutting. At Clonkeen Road, there would have been a bridge with a thirty-five-foot (eleven-metre) span, sixteen feet (five metres) above the road; a smaller bridge would have carried the railway over Pottery Road.[12]

The track would have crossed under Rochestown Avenue and continued in a cutting through what is now the football field south of Sallynoggin, then under the Glenageary Road north of Altidore, before dividing in two just short of Silchester Road – one branch bending northwards to join the Kingstown line near Glengara Park; the south-bound branch swinging south to join it at Glenageary station.[13]

It emerged at the committee that the line would have been just over three miles (five kilometres) in length, and would have had stations at Dean's Grange – no doubt at Clonkeen Road – and at Glenageary Road, as well as at each end, Foxrock and Glenageary. It would, according to the design engineer, be completed for £50,000, although this estimate was disputed by the opponents of the proposal. It was hinted that an agreement had been reached with the Dublin and Wicklow Railway Company for that company to run the railway for 40 per cent of the gross takings.[14]

At an earlier stage, all owners, lessees and occupiers along the route, as well as any potentially interested parties, were notified of the proposal and given an opportunity formally to assent or dissent. Surprisingly, there was generally a lack of response – no response from the Kingstown Town Commissioners, the Dublin and Wicklow Railway Company, the Dublin and Kingstown Railway Company, the County Dublin Grand Jury (predecessors of Dublin County Council), or the Board of Works. Only one landowner, John Crosthwaite, assented; none dissented. Most lessees or occupiers who replied either assented or remained neutral, though the Cunniams of Cornelscourt, whose family were still in the area until recent times, and a man named Byrne, possibly the same Byrne whose house at Primrose Cottage on Westminster Road was to have been demolished, recorded their dissent. The agent for

Georgina Byrne of Cabinteely House did not respond. Lack of formal dissent at this stage was not reflected by lack of opposition later.[15]

William Wellington Bentley, the developer of the Foxrock estate, was the promoters' first witness. He gave some interesting images of the Foxrock of the 1860s. He had been a house agent in Dublin for twenty years and now resided in Foxrock. He stressed the benefits to Foxrock and Dundrum, and to their future development, if the new railway were to be constructed. He owned 500 acres of land in the vicinity, which had been only furze and rocks – a desert – five years previously, and he had invested £40,000 to £50,000 in its development. There were fifty houses on his land and a small hotel, where people came for their health. It was hoped to replace it with a bigger premises. The local people, he said, with only one exception, supported the proposal.[16]

Bentley noted that a Mr Wilson had bought 500 acres in the vicinity and had established a demesne. While Foxrock alone had not sufficient population to support the proposed railway, the population of Dundrum, Milltown and Upper Rathmines needed the service. In 1848, the population of Foxrock was just one herdsman and a couple of hundred sheep and cattle; now there were six or seven people to each house. The railway would itself create traffic. Before the railway came to Dundrum, there was only one omnibus between there and Dublin; now the takings at Foxrock station were £1,000, because people came out to walk around there. There was only one conveyance between Foxrock and Kingstown each day – a car taking six or seven people, which did not always have a full load. In reply to a question he stated, 'The driver blows the horn before he starts but sometimes no passengers show up.'[17]

Indeed, Bentley did not show up very well under cross-examination. The opposing barrister pointed out that the total population of Foxrock was only forty-eight at the last census, and that the population of Dundrum had actually decreased, being now only 487. There were only two shops in Foxrock; a grocer and a provision merchant.[18]

Bentley was followed by William Crowe, a builder, who was at the time operating in Foxrock. He dodged the questions he was given and was quite unimpressive. A number of technical witnesses, railway and civil engineers and land valuers, who indicated their confidence in the proposal, completed the case for the promoters.[19]

For the opponents of the railway, the Earl of Longford appeared in person to express his opposition. There was nothing of a town or even a village in Foxrock; the line would only cut up and disfigure part of his estate to no useful purpose. In particular, he had given a site to the Church of Ireland for a new church at Silchester Road, now St Paul's. Under the proposal, it would be isolated on a triangle between three railway cuttings.[20]

Longford's agent, a Mr Kincaid, contributed further evidence. He indicated that with the dropping of the proposed branch line to the West Pier from the Dublin South Suburban Railway proposal, the Lord now supported *that* proposal. Omnibus services in the area, providing a feeder service to the railways, had not been successful, indicating lack of demand for the new railway. Technical witnesses backed up the laymen's opposition.[21]

Revd Mr Westby, who owned lands at Pottery Road which were listed for acquisition for the line, also claimed that the proposed rail link was unnecessary. Mr James Perry, who owned Clonkeen House, concurred. Perry was embarrassed when a letter he had written some time previously to the railway's promoters was produced, which threatened opposition to the scheme *unless* a station was provided on his land at Cornelscourt, an addition which would have opened up his property for development.[22]

The opposition lawyers, in summing up, slated the proposal. It would only take traffic from the Dublin and Kingstown Railway; there was no population in Foxrock; a car had been substituted for an omnibus because of lack of traffic; the design engineer had never previously built a railway. The promoters stressed the guarantee of success arising from the running arrangement with the Dublin and Wicklow Railway Company and from the potential for opening up the area for development.[23]

At the end of the hearings, the chairman of the committee announced its approval of the proposed link between Kingsbridge and the Harcourt Street Line, and the Ranelagh to Sydney Parade link, but rejected both the South Suburban line and the Foxrock to Kingstown connection. Thus ended the proposal to build a railway link between Foxrock and Kingstown.[24]

Both the inner suburban links survived the subsequent scrutiny of the House of Commons, and secured the Royal Consent in July 1865.[25]

The End of the Boom

As noted earlier, the securing of parliamentary approval for the building of a railway did not necessarily mean that the line would ever be constructed. Although costly to promote a bill in parliament, the step was typically initiated before the financial resources had been assembled. The rush to secure approvals was driven partly by the urge to get a running start over competitors and partly by a wish to capture the investors who were eager to gamble on the long-term success of the railways – the wonders of the day. As in the case of many stock-market booms, the mood soon turned sour and new funds dried up. In 1866, there was only one Dublin railway bill, compared with eleven in 1864, and that sole bill was merely to secure extra time for completing a project which had already been approved.[26]

Indeed, the investment climate had deteriorated so seriously in the late 1860s that there was pressure to nationalise the Irish railways, despite the prevailing political ideology in favour of free enterprise. Of thirty-five railway companies listed on the stock market in 1866, the shares of only one, the Dublin and Kingstown Railway Company, still stood above par.[27]

The Dublin and Wicklow Railway Company, which had secured the approval to build the Ranelagh to Sydney Parade link, suffered a failed stock issue in 1866, and, with the potential competition from both the Dundrum, Foxrock and Kingstown line and from the Dublin South Suburban Railway no longer a threat, they shelved their own proposals. And the other section

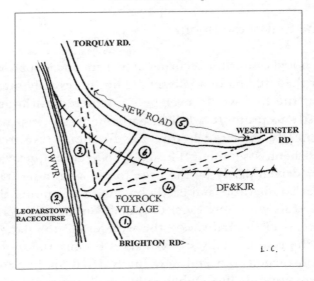

Plan for running a new railway through Foxrock Village: (1) location of today's shops; (2) location of former Foxrock railway station and now entrance to golf range; (3) part of Torquay Road to be closed; (4) part of Westminster Road to be closed; (5) new road to link Torquay and Westminster Roads; (6) level crossing.

How it might have been! An artist's impression of Clonkeen Road, looking north, with the entrance to South Park off picture to the left, the Texaco Garage on the right, and the railway crossing Clonkeen Road near Meadow Vale.

of the approved cross-city link, from the Harcourt Line to Kingsbridge, died when the DRRRR&RR Company, which owned part of that route, failed to get their own main line off the ground.[28]

There is still no east–west railway link across the city. But do not despair. Interconnection is again on the menu, and while there is now no proposal for a central station, some of the connections planned in the 1860s – like the east–west link from Westland Row area to Heuston and a connection between Ranelagh and Broadstone – are again being considered.

So maybe we will yet live to see a DART running between Foxrock and Kingstown – or rather, Dún Laoghaire.

Notes

1 *Dublin Builder* (hereafter *DB*), 1 December 1863, p.191; *DB*, 15 June 1864.

2 *DB*, 1 December 1863, p.191; *DB*, 15 June 1864, pp122-3; *The Irish Times* (hereafter *IT*), 23 November 1864.

3 Larcom Papers, National Library, Ms 7644.

4 *Journal of the House of Commons* (hereafter *JHoC*), Session 1863-4; *The Freeman's Journal* (hereafter *FJ*), 2 December 1864.

5 *JHoC*, Session 1864-5.

6 *FJ*, 22 November 1864; *Dublin Gazette* (hereafter *DG*), 29 November 1864.

7 *FJ* and *IT*, 30 March 1865 to 6 April 1865; *JHoC*, Session 1864-5.

8 *Ibid.*

9 *Ibid.*

10 *Ibid.*; House of Lords, London, manuscript papers related to the Dundrum, Foxrock and Kingstown Junction Railway Bill, 1865; book of reference, plans, minutes of evidence.

11 *Ibid.*

12 *Ibid.*

13 *Ibid.*

14 *Ibid.*

15 *Ibid.*

16 *Ibid.*

17 *Ibid.*

18 *Ibid.*

19 *Ibid.*

20 *Ibid.*

21 *Ibid.*

22 *Ibid.*

23 *Ibid.*

24 *IT*, 6 April 1864.

25 *Journal of the House of Lords*, Session 1864-5.

26 *DG*, 30 November 1866.

27 Joseph Murphy in *Journal of Statistical and Social Inquiry Society of Ireland*, Part xxxii (November 1866), pp307-16.

28 W.E. Shepherd, *The Dublin and South Eastern Railway* (Newtown Abbot, 1974), p.35 et seq.

NB. An act of 1860 renamed the Dublin and Wicklow Railway Company, 'The Dublin, Wicklow and Wexford Railway Company',[28] yet the older title was commonly used in newspapers and other contemporary documents.

6

Foxrock Estate

by Brendan Reynolds (1991)

On a green field site development began on Foxrock Estate in 1859, on lands extending from Brewery Road to Carrickmines crossroads. These lands were purchased by two brothers, William and John Bentley, from the Ecclesiastical Commissioners and Richard Watley, Lord Archbishop of Dublin.

The land then consisted of a great deal of furze and blackthorn bushes, and large amounts of granite rock. It was corralled by the railway on one side and the Bray Road on the other. It was planned to spend £30,000 developing housing sites for sale at £6 to £10 per acre. The Bentleys did build a few large houses and lived in two of them on Brighton Road (Hollymount/ Mountaentine). The first house built on the lands was their estate office on Westminster Road, later converted to a shop and tea rooms by a Mr Byrne and named Picnic Cottage (now Primrose Cottage) by the Welsh Family, who operated the post office and telephone exchange for many years. Byrnes opened the post office in 1870 and the telephone exchange in 1895. With the opening of the new automatic telephone exchange in Dún Laoghaire, the Foxrock exchange closed down. The post office moved to the village in the 1940s.

The Concept of Foxrock in Suburbia

Foxrock was to be a dual-purpose estate, having a holiday resort in what is now the village of Foxrock, where the brothers built a large hotel in 1860, naming it Victoria Hotel and later Tourist Hotel; it was situated near the railway. They requested a station for Foxrock Estate from the railway company, offering £300 towards the cost. The station opened in 1861. It was planned to lay out an ornamental garden with a large lake and play area. They constructed a pleasure garden and a play area consisting of an orchard with apple and pear trees, but the lake was never built. Foxrock was then advertised as renowned for the purity of the air. There must have been some truth in the advertisement, because in later years, when TB was rampant across the country, very few people in the village died from the disease.

The Bentleys sold lime, sand, bricks and cut granite from the local quarries. They built a shopping mart on Albert Road, now Mart Lane, facing out onto the Bray Road, for the purpose of attracting passing trade. One of the first large houses built on Foxrock Estate was Stanford House, Westminster Road. It sold for £800 with ground consisting of a few acres. The first street light was provided on Westminster Road by a Mrs Edmundson, who had her own gasworks in 1862, prior to Foxrock Railway Station opening. The Bentleys provided a coach service to and from Stillorgan and Dún Laoghaire, costing 2*d* and 3*d*. This service continued long after the Bentleys left the area, with week-end trips to the mountains and special trips for residents living on the estate. The stables were situated near Victoria Hotel, on ground now taken over by Foxrock Garage. A Mr Tracey continued on the service using a motor car; a Mr Lynch took it over in the 1930s, and a Bill McCann operated the service up to 1951, moving to St Brigid's Park in 1951. Unfortunately for the Bentley brothers, there was no great rush to purchase housing sites on Foxrock Estate in the 1860s, nor were Dublin dwellers keen to take holidays in the Victoria Hotel. They continued to use the east coast, Dalkey/Bray/Arklow for their vacations. By 1867, the banks were moving in on the developers of Foxrock Estate and the Bentleys moved out. Later, the Royal Insurance Co. purchased the land and it was this company that was responsible for creating the village of Foxrock.

Foxrock Village

When Royal Exchange Insurance took over Foxrock Estate they had in their possession the old hotel, then many years vacant. Having realised that staff were required by the owners of the big houses on the estate, they decided to convert it into accommodation for the working-class people. In 1879, fourteen families moved in. They came mostly from the country – Kildare, Wexford, Wicklow, etc. – and took up employment as gardeners, coachmen and dairymen on the estate. Extra living accommodation was provided in the village in

1901. Eight dwellings were built in the orchard and named Orchard Cottages, and a further twelve were built and named Brighton Cottages. Compared to the old hotel, these cottages were considered luxurious, with large gardens, indoor water taps and their own toilets. They were designed to face the railway line, as most of the traffic passing through Foxrock went by rail. The rear of the houses was nicely obscured from Brighton Road, with trees and two rows of hedging. By the year 1910, there were thirty-four families living in the village. The cottages were given to the residents of the big houses on the estate for the use of their employees, though this arrangement did not always suit the villageers, because if you lost your job, you also lost your home. The practice was discontinued in the 1930s, as residents of the cottages refused to leave their homes.

The first shop opened in the village at No. 1 Brighton Cottages, followed by a shop at No. 11 Brighton

The old post office, Foxrock. Originally the Estate Office, it is now called Primrose Cottage.

Cottages. A Mr MacEvoy and a Mrs Lynch were the proprietors. In 1906, Alex Findlater opened his shop adjacent to the railway station.

To cater for sightseers at the weekends, two tea shops opened at No.2 and No.3 Orchard Cottages. Proprietors were Mrs Foran and Mrs Sharp. Some time later, a Mr Tully opened a dairy at No.12 Brighton Cottages. Most of the villagers kept hens and goats. In 1910, a temporary church was erected on Torquay Road to cater for the village residents. Cabinteely had been their parish church, built in 1836. The Church of Ireland opened in 1862 on Brighton Road.

Origin of the name Foxrock

The name Foxrock was used in the area in 1810 to name a house on the Bray Road. In 1840, a Mr Quigley gave his address as 'Fox Rock'. I was told that the Quigley family lived near the village in a squatters' dwelling on Westminster Road.

In my young days, there were lots of foxes around and also plenty of granite rock. A granite slab lay for many years outside the old estate office, now Primrose Cottage. A fox's head could be observed on it and so residents in the village believed the name derived from this stone. My guess is that it was cut out of the local quarries, and the fox's head carved out by one of the Bentleys' stonemasons who worked the quarries, cutting out stone windowsills. Remains of one of the granite quarries can still be seen in the village. The fox-rock stone was removed to the village in 1969.

Leopardstown

Leopardstown was another source of income. Baile Na Lobar, or Lepers' Town, was once part of a leper colony; it was an extension of Stephen's Hospital, which was built on land where Mercer's Hospital now stands. Baile Na Lobar served those stricken with disease and continued in use up to the seventeenth century. In 1867, a branch of the Benedictine Fathers was told to leave France by the French Government. This group travelled to Ireland and set up an Agricultural College on the lands of Leopardstown. They remained in the area for sixteen years, leaving in 1882 to travel to England to take over Buckfast Abbey. The college had created a great deal of employment in the area and so it was a great disappointment to the locals when it closed down.

Six years later, the racecourse opened and the villagers supplemented their incomes by taking in jockeys and stable boys, giving them overnight accommodation. This practice continued up to the 1950s. An eighteen-hole golf course was laid out on the grounds in 1891, but closed a year later. In 1893, the Royal Exchange opened a nine-hole course off Torquay Road.

First World War

With the outbreak of war, young men in the village were encouraged by their employers to join the British Army. About eight men out of the village took up arms and three died in action.

Prior to the war, the locals showed great allegiance to the Royal Family. King Edward VII visited Leopardstown Racecourse in 1904, and King George V made a visit in 1911. Foxrock village was decorated with flags and coloured bunting for the occasion. This loyal support was to change later.

For the duration of the war, people were encouraged to grow food, and Rathdown District Council sought land for the families living in the old hotel. They corresponded with some local landowners – Sir Horace Plunkett, Foxrock Golf Club, Boss Croker and others – but no land was made available. A small number of residents used the railway banks and they also grazed their goats there.

War of Independence

With the outbreak of the war, Foxrock village was considered to be a camp for the local IRA, and while on the run, members stayed overnight in the cottages and sometimes in the old hotel. Following the shooting of Constable Skeet in 1921, and later, a British soldier in Foxrock, the Black and Tans stationed in Cabinteely carried out many raids in to seek out the local IRA. In one of these raids, a local lad, Thomas Murphy, was shot in the presence of his mother. The family lived in the old hotel. Their father, who was deceased, had been a member of the British Army and had fought in the Boer War.

Michael Collins' Spy in Dublin Castle

David Neligan, a double agent investigating the killing of military homing pigeons at Foxrock railway station, described Foxrock then as a pleasant and quiet country place. While looking around Foxrock, he was approached by the local IRA and taken into old stables nearby for questioning. He told them he was an insurance man and, without searching him, they released him. In his possession he had a .38 revolver, a curfew pass issued only to special agents, and an anonymous letter received in Dublin Castle with a Foxrock postmark describing the pigeon killers. He reckoned that these items, if found, were a passport to a better world.

The Civil War

With the outbreak of the Civil War, most of the village took the republican side, and the armed struggle continued in Foxrock, this time in opposition to the Irish Free State Government. The locals started their campaign with the burning of the railway signal cabin in Foxrock station, destroyed the local telephone switchboard, burnt down Sir Horace Plunkett's mansion on Westminster Road and robbed the post office. A Mr John Jones was shot while on a visit to his brother in Foxrock. Michael Collins' convoy was fired on after he had paid a visit to Sir Horace Plunkett's home.

A question was asked in Dáil Éireann by Mr D. Figgis and put to Mr Mulcahy, Defence Minister, 'What steps are being taken to safeguard people living in Foxrock who are being terrorised night and day?' His reply was that it was intended to set up a military post on the grounds of Leopardstown. Some time later, two men were arrested and two shot dead by the Free State Army in New Park Lodge, Bray Road.

Second World War

My memories go back to the Second World War. An unforgettable incident occurred when a British Beaufighter aeroplane was observed flying around for some time before crashing into the boundary wall of Leopardstown. Most of the village people appeared at the scene of the crash to find the crew standing around, waiting for ambulances to come. They had received only small cuts to their arms and faces. We took many bits and pieces of the plane back home with us. The next plane landed in Leopardstown after going short of fuel. It was a USA C-47. It refuelled during the night and took off the next day. We had unauthorised leave from school that day. I remember looking into the plane before it took off and seeing bananas for the first time, hanging up inside.

We listened to the war news on our two-valve radio; to 'Lord Haw-Haw' broadcasting from Germany. He had a beautiful speaking voice. I was told he was from Galway. I remember his last broadcast, which sounded as if it had been made under the influence of liquor. Later, I followed his court case, which led to his execution. Only the British Government took him seriously. We had no licence for our radio and we used our clothes-line wire for the aerial and like many other radios in the village it was hidden away during the daytime.

Garden plots were provided in the village for residents in the old hotel on the old Rock Rovers' Hockey Pitch and it became a great meeting place for the locals.

I can remember the beautiful trees growing around Foxrock Estate and we were familiar with the sweet chestnut and walnut tree. Many trees disappeared overnight and everyone had great fires burning during the winter months. We made many visits to Findlater's shop to see the overhead rail carrying the money to the cash office, and to the local post office and telephone exchange to observe the working of the old National Telephone Switchboard. There were three workshops in the old hotel yard. A Mr Murphy had a woodworking shop, Mr Dignam repaired bicycles and Mr Robinson repaired boots and shoes. The village then seemed to be self-contained. Race day in Leopardstown created a great atmosphere. We finished the day watching the stable boys endeavouring to return the race horses to the railway boxes at Foxrock Station. Horses' hooves flew in all directions.

Winston Churchill Letter Arrives in the Village

A Mr Norris, who lived in the village, told me about the many battles he took part in as a member of the British Army and one of them was the famous Battle of Omdurman. Three Victoria Crosses were awarded after the battle. The British were on the way to relieve Khartoum in Sudan. Churchill had told the press he was the only one alive that took part in the famous Battle of Omdurman.

Mr Norris wrote to Churchill, informing him that he also took part in the battle. Churchill wrote back and included a book he had written of his memoirs.

We spent many happy days as caddies on Foxrock Golf Course, where we received one penny a hole and played golf after hours without permission. We found lost golf balls and sold them back to members.

Gas company inspectors called many times to check if people were using the gas during certain hours. 'The glimmer man', as he was called, was followed around by the local children, much to his annoyance. The element of surprise, therefore, was taken from him.

Sam Beckett's mother used to pass through the village by ass and trap, with her not-too-friendly dog sitting up beside her. She was considered a tough woman to work for. Her son Sam appeared after the war and wrote a play, *All that Fall*. Local people got a mention: Mr Farrell (station master), Mr Shannon (whistling postman), Mr Tully (local milkman) and Mr Thomas Postman (Welcome Home Master – a greeting he used). Places also mentioned were the bog (wetland in the village) and Orchard Cottage (Slum Cottage).

Foxrock Geraldines Football Club restarted in 1947, having being disbanded in the 1930s. The formation of this club dates back to a few years after the GAA was founded.

The Villages Move Out

With the building of St Brigid's Park in the 1950s, residents moved out of the old hotel to the new dwellings in Cornelscourt. The Victoria Hotel was demolished some years later by a local man, P. Thomson. There had been great opposition to the building of St Brigid's Park, resulting in roadside public meetings in support of the new estate.

The Harcourt Street Railway closed in 1958. Findlater's shop and another grocery shop closed in the village, but elsewhere on Foxrock Estate, the building of housing estates was taking place and people were moving in at a fast rate.

The village has changed a great deal with the building of Foxrock Lodge, the development of a small estate on the old orchard land, and the erection of large two-storey houses on the Old Victoria Hotel grounds. The 1926 telephone kiosk still stands in the village, a reminder of the days when it was the only telephone available for use by villagers.

My family moved into the village in 1928 and my father worked for Panters of Kerrymount Avenue. His father also worked in Foxrock. He came from Wicklow. We were known as 'Panter Reynolds' to distinguish us from other Reynolds families in the village, nicknamed 'Gosh' and 'Battey' Reynolds. The last of my family left Foxrock in 1984.

7

The Story of Cornelscourt

by Ted Farrell (1985)

The Original Name of the Village

Cornelscourt Town, as it was called, when first defined, rather loosely, in the Census returns for 1901, embraces part of two townlands: Cornelscourt and Foxrock. It includes Foxrock Mart (now Sexton's Garden Centre) to the north and extends to the gate into the football field on the southern side of the village.

Cornelscourt is not the original name of the village. Many variations appear in published maps and reports, including Cornellston, Cornerstown, Cornelyscort, Cornettscourt, Cornerescourt and Villa Corner, the last two being the earliest names mentioned. They appear in the Account Roll of the Priory of the Holy Trinity, Christ Church, for the year 1326.

At the end of the Middle Ages, nearly 50 per cent of the land in County Dublin was held by the Church. Christ Church, that is the priory of the Holy Trinity, was one of the principal ecclesiastical landowners in the county, holding 10,538 acres. This land was administered by the priory as several large manors. It included the present townland of Foxrock, which was part of the manor of Clonkeen.

There is some confusion, however, over Cornelscourt, in which, at that time, Cabinteely was included. The Account Roll of the Priory of the Holy Trinity for 1326 states that Gregory Taunton held one and a half acres in the vicinity of 'Crowhans by Cornerescourt'. He also held 'Cornerescourt', the manor house, on an annual lease. It seems, therefore, that he did not hold all of the lands of Cornelscourt but only the manor house (a subsidiary manor of Clonkeen) and a few acres around it.

It is likely that the lands of Cornelscourt were held from about the middle of the thirteenth century by the nuns of the House of the Trinity at Lismullen in Meath, and it is here that we get a clue to the origin of the name of the village. Certainly, at the Dissolution of the Monasteries in the 1540s, Cornelscourt was held by the nuns at Lismullen. It is impossible to trace exactly when or how they acquired this land, but it is significant that the first prioress at Lismullen was Avice de la Cornere. Furthermore, the priory was founded by her brother, the Bishop of Meath, Richard de la Cornere, about the year 1250. Richard endowed the new priory with lands from his possessions in Meath and Dublin, including a rift of land in a place called 'Ballygodman', the location of which is no longer known but which, it is clear from other sources, was in south County Dublin and apparently quite close to the manor of Clonkeen. Ballygodman may well correspond to the present townland of Cornelscourt or, more likely, with the combined townlands of Cornelscourt and Cabinteely. Richard had an illegitimate son, William. It is interesting to speculate that, to avoid any embarrassment, he was set up in the manor of Cornelscourt, far from his father's diocese. The land was given to the priory of Lismullen, but the manor was perhaps retained in the family until it passed into the possession of Christ Church in the fourteenth century, before finally falling to the Lismullen nuns, who owned the surrounding land, some time between then and the Dissolution in the sixteenth century.

Whatever the merits of this hypothesis, it does appear likely that the manor house was associated with the Cornere family and that the original name was Cornerescourt.

Farrell's shop, Cornelscourt.

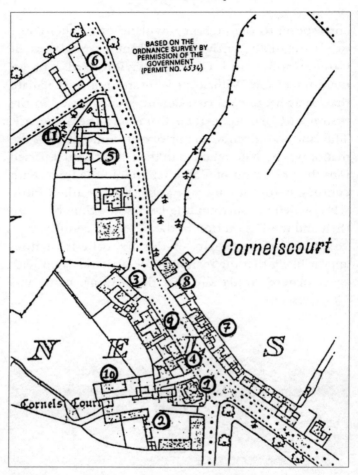

Map of Cornelscourt.

The Castle at Cornelscourt

The so-called castle at Cornelscourt was probably little more than a manor house. The name 'court' suggests a manor house and may also imply a courtyard, an enclosure. The standard Norman fortified structure was a motte and bailey castle, a stockaded tower on the summit of a manmade hill, surrounded by a ditch at the base. Many knights, however, could not afford such a costly structure and had to be satisfied with a manor house surrounded by a wooden stockade and possibly a moat for protection.

It is possible that the original building was improved and strengthened by the addition of a tower, probably in the fourteenth or fifteenth century. Certainly, at the Dissolution of the priory of Lismullen in 1540, the structure at Cornelscourt was called a castle and there was a specific reference to a tower. A hundred years later, in the Civil Survey, the castle is described as having a thatched roof – not suggestive of a structure primarily defensive in nature. In 1781 there is reference to a 'mean old castle, the lower part one continued arch and the upper, open and ruinous,' and in 1838, John Dalton tells us that 'the stump of its ancient castle yet remains'.

In 1850, the last remnant of the castle still stood, behind the site where the house, Bridgemount (see No. 1 on map), was built in the early years of the twentieth century. At that time, the village consisted of a few houses set back from the road on the western side of the present village. I believe that this group of cottages represents the relict court settlement, the cluster of cabins around the old manor house. There were eight cottages there in 1846. Interestingly, in 1545, there were also eight cottages, while Austin Cooper in 1781 says merely that 'there are some cabins adjoining the castle'. By 1900, only two of these cottages, both at Cunniam's farm (No.2 on map), remained and no trace of the others has been found.

The Modern Settlement

There were ten households in the village in 1850, all located on the western side of the road. In addition to the eight cottages, a house, much smaller than the present structure, stood on the site of the pub (No.3 on map) and a woman named Sarah Byrne lived in or beside the new Cabinteely National School (No.4 on map), which had opened in 1844. This building now houses a Chinese restaurant. The other, older schoolhouse at the Clonkeen (No.5 on map) was closed at that time. Of the ten families in 1846, there were three Byrnes and two Cunniams, and the others were O'Brien, Doyle, McCabe, Flynn and Tannam. The Cunniams, who farmed the land on the northern side of Cornelscourt Hill (known as Cunniam's Hill locally) survived until 1975, when the last member, Mick, died. We know little about the other families. Surprisingly, by 1855, most of the cottages had changed hands.

The present pub was a farmhouse in 1846, occupied by Nicholas Byrne. In 1862, John Byrne, a farmer, was head of the household. Patrick Byrne opened a grocery business there about that time, later adding a public house. Three of Patrick's daughters appear in the records of the school in the 1870s.

Shortly after Patrick Byrne set up his business, George F. Collins, my great-grandfather, moved into

Foxrock Mart (No.6 on map), now Sexton's. The Mart was built between 1860 and 1864 as part of the Foxrock Estate, then under development by William Wellington Bentley and John Bentley. Collins started a grocery business with an off licence. For a while he tried selling meat but he soon gave this up. The diaries he kept from 1864 to 1904 give a real feel for life in the village at that time. They tell of a community close to the soil, directly dependent on animals for milk, meat and transport. Interestingly, Cornelscourt is never mentioned over the forty years of entries. It does appear in another book which he kept to record the deaths of friends and neighbours, as well as national and international figures. In noting the death of Patrick Byrne, he displays a keen awareness of the townland boundary which crosses the main road immediately to the north of the pub. Patrick Byrne, therefore, is listed as coming from Cornelscourt. The Mart, on the other hand, is always described as being in Foxrock, which indeed it is. The same awareness of the townland boundaries is shown in the school records of the time. Children from the Clonkeen – the group of cottages between the pub and the Mart Lane – are described as coming from Foxrock; Patrick Byrne's three daughters from Cornelscourt.

By 1901, the village had taken on its present shape and most of the buildings which exist today had been erected. The population of Cornelscourt townland in 1851 was eighty; perhaps fifty people in the village itself, living in ten houses. By 1901, the village had spread over the townland boundary into Foxrock. The population of the village had risen to 160 and the number of houses to thirty-one.

The Village Develops

After Patrick Byrne's death in February 1891, the pub
was taken over by Bernard Rogan. He and his wife,
Bridget, were then in their mid-thirties. The Rogan
family held the pub until about 1915. Bernard Rogan
is responsible for the village as it appears today. It was
he who, in the period 1894-1901, built the first seven
cottages in the Clonkeen (No.5 on map) and then the
fourteen on the eastern side of the main road (No.7
on map). The Rogans also had a butcher's stall at the
northern end of the pub and later built a butcher's shop
(No.8 on map), across the road, beside what is now
Gordyn's shop.

In 1901, by far and away the most common
occupation among the inhabitants of the village was
that of agricultural labourer. There were twenty-three
of them. In addition, there were six national teachers
and a monitress. Annie O'Farrell was the principal of
the girls' school. She lived in the teachers' house nearest
the school (No.9 on map). This and the other teachers'
house, which adjoined it, were built by the parish in
the 1880s. Her niece, eighteen-year-old Mary Jane
Lowbridge, a monitress, and Kate Cassidy, assistant
teacher, also lived in the same house. Andrew O'Farrell,
who was principal of the boys' school from 1883
to 1900, was the first occupant of the other teachers'
house. In 1901, his successor, John O'Regan, lived there.
O'Regan's wife, Annie, was also a school teacher, and
living with them was another teacher, twenty-one-
year-old, Hugh McCambridge. Finally, Mary Kate
Farrell, my grandmother, who lived at the Mart, made

the daily journey by train from Foxrock station to
Harcourt Street to her job as principal of the Carmelite
School at Whitefriar Street.

Other occupations represented in the village include
those of butcher, clerk, grocer's assistant, stonecutter,
laundress, gardener and domestic servant (often the
two were combined), van driver, carpenter, dressmaker,
dairywoman, groom, builder's labourer, coachman,
shoemaker, bricklayer and general labourer. There
were no gentlemen's residences in the village, and in
1901 there was just one family of Protestants – Joshua
Kearney, a thirty-year-old carpenter who lived in the
cottages with his sisters, Louise and Frances, and who
belonged to the Church of Ireland.

A large number of people lived at the Mart (No.6 on
map) at least up to the mid-1890s, although none were
there for the census of 1901. Why they lived there I don't
know. Some were National School teachers. Michael
Connolly, who moved from the schoolhouse to the Mart
in 1881, was dismissed from his post as teacher in 1883.
A music teacher called Kennedy lived there and gave
lessons to the Collins girls, but the occupations of most
of the others are a mystery.

The lodgers in Foxrock Mart in the 1864-1890 period
came and went extraordinarily frequently and similar
activity was exhibited by the early tenants of Rogan's
cottages. In the first few years after they were built, there
were many changes of tenancy in the fourteen cottages
on the eastern side of the road. I cannot be certain of
continuity in any of them through to 1950. However,
some families, while they may have moved from one
cottage to another, did live there for most of these fifty

years. The Lynch family lived in No. 13. The Census of
1911 lists Andrew, who at that time was forty years of
age, and his wife, Margaret. Of their children, the three
eldest, Paddy, Tom and Andy, were some of the best-
known men in the locality in my early years, and I'm
glad to say that many of their children still live locally
and are among the genuine old stock of Cornelscourt.
Next door to them, in No. 12, lived the McCanns. John
McCann was twenty-eight years of age in 1901. He was
an agricultural labourer, a descendant of another John
McCann who was executed for his part in the rising of
1798. Sadly, by 1911, John McCann was dead, leaving his
widow, Mary, to raise four children. Another branch of
the McCann family lived in the old schoolhouse in the
Clonkeen (No. 5 on map). In 1911, there were twelve in
that household. Also in the Clonkeen were the Kirwans
and the Quigleys, the last of whom, Simon, lived there
until his death a number of years ago. Their house was
demolished some months ago.

The first half of the twentieth century saw
Cornelscourt develop into a real village for quite a short
period – perhaps twenty or thirty years – followed by
a slow decline to 1950, where my story stops. Indeed, I
chose 1950 as my end point because the construction
of St Brigid's Park in 1952, while greatly improving
the living conditions of many people, disrupted the old
community and fundamentally altered the character of
the village.

Bridgemount (No. 1 on map), at the end of the village,
was built in the early years of the twentieth century.
The famous jockey Steve Donoghue was one of the
first occupants, probably from the time he got married,

towards the end of 1908, until he went to work with the Atty Persse stables at Chattis Hill, near Stockbridge in Hampshire, in the latter half of 1910.

By that time the butcher's shop (No.8 on map) was in business. It was operated first by the Rogan family, who offered it for sale in 1913, then by Joseph Doyle, until it was bought by Pat Farrell, who owned Farrell's butchers in Cabinteely, in 1919. The inventory of the premises, at that stage, included a slaughter house, stables, two bicycles, a refrigerator (out of order), a pony and van, fifteen ewes, a one-and-a-half-year-old bullock, three tons of hay and an unspecified quantity of manure. Pat Farrell did not stay in business in Cornelscourt for very long, because by 1922 the building was no longer in use as a butcher. Tom Gilleran, a champion cyclist and a Free Stater, and Frank McDonald, reputedly an IRA man, formed an unlikely partnership and set up what was originally a bicycle repair shop, on the ground floor of the butcher. The few car owners in the area started to go there, so the business gradually began to develop, and by 1922 it was known as Foxrock Cycle and Motor Works. After the butcher's shop closed, one of the staff (possibly Mick Brennan from Cabinteely) set up business in the old stall against the pub, which at this stage was owned by Willie Connolly. This did not last long either, however, because in 1921 or 1922, it was demolished by a runaway car.

Following the destruction of Cabinteely barracks during the Civil War in July 1922, the Commissioners of Public Works took out a lease on the upper floor of Pat Farrell's former butcher's shop, at that point the bicycle shop. The three rooms there were used as the barracks. They also leased the Foresters' Hall (No. 10 on map), which was located some thirty yards off the road, between the old school and Bridgemount. They moved back to Cabinteely about 1926.

By 1927, Gilleran and McDonald's business had expanded and they built what is now Cornelscourt Garage. The butcher's shop was neglected and only a sad ruin remains today.

Economic Life

The commercial life of the village was quite considerable. Besides the two grocery businesses, the pub, the butcher and later the garage, there was a sweet shop in the Lynch cottage (No. 13) in the 1920s. The Robinsons, who lived in the Clonkeen (No. 5 on map),

The old St Brigid's Schoolhouse, Cornelscourt.

were all bootmakers and carried on a business from their house. The Cunniams sold milk from their farm and the two Misses Cunniam, Lil and Polly, were both dressmakers. The Clares were builders and had a sawmill in what is now the car park of the Magic Carpet.

Friendly societies have played an important role in the economic life of the village, meeting a social need and providing a form of insurance against sickness and the economic losses of bereavement. Organisations whose existence I have traced in the village include the Foresters, the South County Dublin Loan Society, Foxrock Investment Loan Society and the Tontine Society.

The Irish National Foresters entered into a lease in 1914 for a plot of land (No.10 on map) behind the old school (the present Chinese restaurant), where they erected a hall – a galvanised-iron structure. It became a great centre of activity in the village and was the scene of many a dance, film and political gathering. It was also used by the South County Dublin Loan Society. Nearby, the school, which was vacated with the move to St Brigid's in 1914, became the living quarters for teachers, principally the Collins family. Jerry Collins was a teacher in the boys' school from 1903 to 1950 or 1951. He moved to the old school in Cornelscourt in 1914 and he and his wife brought up their family there.

The Ancient Order of Hibernians also appear in the village, in a hut located in the 'plantation' (No.11 on map), the grove of trees opposite the back entrance to Sextons. The origin of this hut is interesting. In the early 1900s, my grandfather Ted Farrell, brother of Pat the butcher, was dying of TB. He was sent to Kimberley, in South Africa, where he made a spectacular recovery.

On his return to Ireland, he lived, on medical instruction, in a wooden hut located in the back garden of the Mart. Later, the hut was resited in the plantation. It was long a haunt for drinkers who bought their supplies in the Mart. It was also leased by the AOH from 1915 until 1932. In addition, the Tontine Society functioned in the hut.

Decline

The outbreak of the Second World War brought considerable changes to the village. The Foresters' Hall went into decline. The LDF, forerunners of the FCA, took it over for training, but the old wooden floor was not up to the tramp of marching feet. They moved to the garage (then closed because there were no cars) where they remained until the end of the war. Tim O'Reilly set up business there in 1946.

I do not know when the AOH disappeared from the village. Indeed, I am struck by how small a part my own recollections play in this story. I am inclined to forget that my history ends thirty-five years ago. I do have a few memories, however, and I shall conclude with them. How many people, I wonder, remember the marvellous day in the late 1940s when a plane landed in the field opposite Farrell's shop? I remember it quite vividly. It was a small private plane, the fuselage was blue, and I watched with a child's wonder from an upper window as it took off and banked steeply over the house. I remember, too, a column of soldiers marching through the village; their green uniforms and the tramp of their boots.

And I remember a circus, where in the innocence of those pre-television days, people performed magic and a man tied himself in knots before my trusting eyes. I am delighted to see Fossett's Circus performing in the village now and I love to bring my children there to the big top in the field that my grand-uncle Pat Farrell bought, along with fifteen ewes and a bullock, in 1919.

Acknowledgements

Liam Clare was the inspiration of my work; gently but persistently prodding me into action and very helpfully directing me to valuable sources.

In the Department of Medieval History in UCD, Dr Art Cosgrove helped me with medieval records and Dr Howard Clarke gave me invaluable assistance on the origin of the name of the village and the nature of the castle. Dr Fergus D'Arcy, in Modern History, helped me greatly on the nineteenth-century period and was a source of inspiration to me. I am deeply grateful to them all.

Finally, this work would be nothing without the help of the men and women of Cornelscourt who shared their memories with me. In particular I must mention the late Mrs Seville, the Misses Dot, Tess and Pal McCann, Mrs Andy Lynch, Fintan Flynn, Sean McCann, Andy Seville, Michael Sinnott and Donie Collins.

References and Further Reading

Primary Printed Sources

Pre-1800:

Calendar of Documents Relating to Ireland, 1171-1251, 1252-1272, 1285-1292.

Calendar of Patent Rolls, Henry III, 6, 1266-1272; Edward III, 14, 1367-1370.

Civil Survey, 1654-1656, County of Dublin, Vol. II, Stationery Office, Dublin (1945).

McNeill, Charles (ed.), Calendar of Archbishop Alen's Register, *c.*1172-1534 (1950).

Mills, James, Account Roll of the Priory of the Holy Trinity, Dublin, 1337-1346 (1891).

Rawlinson Manuscripts, Analetica Hibernica, pp121-2 (1930).

Reports of Deputy Keeper of Public Records, 1888-1895.

Christchurch Deeds, Appendices to Reports 20-7.

White, Newport B., *Extents of Irish Monastic Possessions, 1540-1541* (1943).

1800-1950:

Census of Ireland, 1841 to 1946; Detailed returns, 1901 and 1911.

Commissioners of Irish Education Enquiry, Second Report, 1826.

Ferrell, E.P., *Diaries of G.F. Collins*, UCD Archives.

Landed Estate Court Records, 1870, W.W. Bentley, 96/18.

Thom's Directory, 1860-1950.

Valuation Office, Field Books, 1846; Primary Valuation, 1846, and Subsequent Valuations.

Secondary Sources

Bell, F.E., *A History of the County Dublin, Part 1* (1902).

Cronin, P., *A History of the Parish of Foxrock* (Foxrock Local History Club, 1984).

Dalton, J., *The History of Co. Dublin* (1838).

Gosden, P.H., *Self Help* (1973).

McGowan, E., *St Brigid's School, Foxrock* (Foxrock Local History Club, 1981).

Otway-Ruthven, A.J., 'The Medieval Church Lands of County Dublin', in *Medieval Studies* presented to Aubrey Gwynn, SJ (Watt, J.A., Morrell, J.B., & Martin, F.X. (eds), 1961), pp54-73.

Otway-Ruthven, A.J., *A History of Medieval Ireland* (1980).

Price, L. (ed.), *An Eighteenth-Century Antiquary, The sketches, notes and diaries of Austin Cooper* (1759-1830) (1942).

St John Joyce, W., *The Neighbourhood of Dublin* (1912).

8

Sea Baths of South County Dublin

by Seán Quinn (2001)

Earlier History

Great civilisations highly valued bathing. The Romans had a passion for bathing, and building magnificent baths, often with markets and libraries adjoining. These were real leisure and social centres, noted for beautiful mosaics and marbles. Maecenas is said to have built the first heated swimming pool in the first century BC; Japan had compulsory school swimming in AD 1603. The Roman baths in the English spa town of Bath have lasted some two millennia, and following recent major refurbishment, have taken on a new lease of life. It is rightly treasured by the authorities and jealously preserved. It has links with Ireland — the Celts arrived first, and their god Sul was linked by the Romans to Minerva, their god of healing, to ensure a sustainable development. In Ireland, our ancestors also treasured bathing, especially for therapeutic purposes, and stories recall warriors bathing their wounds in the healing waters of the sea.

Old maps of the South Dublin Coast show numerous bathing places, rock pools and baths. Bath Street in Irishtown had bathing boxes along the strand. Murphy's baths in Ringsend are mentioned, but there is no trace now. Wolfe Tone, who lived in Ringsend, was a frequent swimmer nearby, where he had a bathing box. Irishtown, at a place marked by a commemoration stone, was the scene of the 'Waxies' Dargle', renowned in song and story. Houses are now built there, on reclaimed land.

Cranfield Baths: Well Ahead of their Time

In 1791, Richard Cranfield, a wood carver and builder, built his public baths, claimed to be the first in Ireland, complete with 'unlimited supplies of pure sea water'. Open seven months of the year, it housed extensive facilities, including overnight accommodation. The site has been redeveloped for housing and no trace of the once-famous baths remains today.

The baths, which were on the seashore, are recorded in a local street name, Cranfield Place, and were situated between Tritonville Avenue and Leahy Terrace. The baths were a well-known and fashionable institution in Dublin, well ahead of their time. Daniel O'Connell mentions an early morning swim there before he set out from the South Wall for parliament in London. The baths are linked to the present day by the Dublin Swimming Club, which held its galas there in the 1880s. Mr Cranfield died in 1859 and is buried in St Matthew's church, Irishtown, where his grave can be seen.

Pembroke (Merrion/Sandymount) Baths

Near the Martello Tower on Sandymount Strand, these baths were also privately owned. They were built in 1880 and lasted until the 1920s. Sandymount already had great fame as a watering place, with hotels, lodging houses and the famous 'Conniving House' pub. The remains of the once elegant sea baths still rise forlornly on Sandymount Strand. When the Pembroke Estate approved the development, existing licences for bathing facilities on the strand were rescinded, causing consternation to the families affected. The baths were linked to the shore by a fifty-yard Victorian cast-iron pier or causeway. Band recitals, minstrel shows, and fancy-dress events took place regularly. 'Penny dry, half-penny wet,' and 'you get what you pay for,' phrases referring to hiring bathing costumes, are still sometimes heard locally.

Blackrock Baths: Town's Days of Glory

Blackrock, once part of the city, was always popular with Dubliners. In the early 1700s – in pre-Victorian days – we read 'how large bathing parties frequented the 'Rock,' with a 'suggestion that men and women went swimming in the nude'. In 1754, a public subscription was sought to provide a better swimming place in Blackrock. The Peafield Baths, which was located on the site of the Park Keeper's Lodge, and near the site of the 'the rock', were very popular, and a row of bathing boxes stood on the shore. Carriages converged on Blackrock, then as popular as 'the most popular street in the city'. The town's facilities were well patronised throughout the eighteenth century. Lord Edward Fitzgerald arrived at Frascati House as a child in 1767 and enjoyed the local clean air, sandy beaches and swimming; the focus of his education was sea bathing. He wrote to his 'Dearest Mama' of how he 'loved the sea at Blackrock'. The gentry were then flocking to the sea at fashionable Blackrock: Lord Cloncurry at his Maretimo demesne, Sir Harcourt Lees at Blackrock House, Ms Fitzmaurice at Valhalla Gardens (where Lios an Uisce now stands), Lord Clonmel at Temple Lodge. Clearly, the place to be – the 'Gold Coast' of Ireland!

The foreshore at Maretimo still has the eighteenth-century remains of the hexagonal brick building with gothic windows, part of a complex of bathing houses and enclosed seawater pool. A handsome tower bridge, built by the railway company to allow access from the estate to the foreshore, still graces the scene, also the little Doric temple remains of a once extensive boathouse. Vances Harbour, at the rear of Blackrock House, was the venue for the Blackrock swimming races organised by the Blackrock Swimming Club. A festive occasion there in 1880, with two bands, was marred by a tragic drowning.

The Dublin Kingstown Railway, built in 1834, had a major physical impact on the coast line – the railway embankment cut across the strand to Blackrock, leaving numerous swimming places high and dry.

To assuage swimmers cut off by the railway in 1834 from their traditional places, and no doubt with an eye for business, the railway company, on foot of a lease from the Earl of Pembroke, arranged for new baths to be built alongside the station. It was a success story from the start, popular with locals and visitors alike. The years 1874/5 saw brilliant summers. Well-attended water festivals, music proms and polo matches took place. However, fierce storms came in 1887 and battered the baths into the sea. They were soon rebuilt 'in concrete cement', with seating and an adjoining prom. The newly established Irish Amateur Swimming Association (IASA) helped the local authority in continuing the success story. The authority purchased the baths in 1926 and set about a major refurbishment, helped by IASA – an ideal partnership arrangement! – providing for over one thousand spectators, a fifty-metre, eight-lane, Olympic-style pool, and ten-metre and five-metre high-board diving platforms, all in readiness for the successful Tailtean Games held in 1928, attended by the world's leading swimmers. The Blackrock Baths success story continued with such stars as Eddie Heron, who was men's High-Board Diving Champion in every year from 1933 to 1950 and today is remembered by a plaque on the railway bridge in Blackrock. For some fifty years, the baths hosted full-scale international swimming, water polo and diving galas all summer long. While water polo clubs continued to use the baths for some time, they were closed by the local authority in the mid-1980s. Like many others, I have happy memories of the baths, where I fell in love with a different girl every day!

Polo in the sea baths at Blackrock.

Seapoint Baths at Brighton Vale

The owners of baths at Williamstown, left high and dry
by the new railway, were given new baths here. They
opened in 1849 and were very fashionable, particularly in
the 1920s with galas and fun days. The Dublin Swimming
Club held their summer races there in 1875: 'very
colourful events, most light-hearted festive atmosphere'.

Originally forming one premises, they were later
divided in two. There were sea-bathing baths with
iron posts which carried a pier, as well as a chute
pointing into the sea. These baths had a shop and
tearooms attached. In the adjoining building, there
were enclosed hot seawater baths. The baths closed in
1962 and now contain private dwellings. The Seapoint
Swimmers, a group of year-round swimmers, continue

to enjoy the sea at the Martello Tower, where some facilities are provided.

Dún Laoghaire Baths: Jewel in the Crown

The first baths were built by a Mr Hayes in 1828, for the patrons of his Royal Hotel. Kingstown was fast becoming a popular resort. In 1843, John Crosthwaite obtained government approval to provide public baths on the coastal battery site, which was no longer needed as the Napoleonic threat of invasion was over. The new baths, excellently situated, fronting on to Queen's Road, opposite the People's Park, were called the Royal Victoria Baths. Mr Crosthwaite also built baths in Salthill in the 1850s. In 1892, we read how successful the new Kingtown Baths were:

> Frequented by large numbers of the local elite as well as by all classes of tourists and families, for whom there is provided the best of accommodation and attention ... attentiveness and modest charges ... families provided with all the privileges of seabathing without obtrusiveness ... impossible to describe the abundant comforts that are placed in the way of Ladies and Gentlemen ... Baths could not be more favourably located as one of Kingstown's permanent acquisitions.

At the turn of the century, the baths were acquired by Kingston UDC, who undertook major refurbishment between 1905 and 1911. It reopened in 1907 and the good times continued. The sea baths were the pride of the people, the envy of outsiders and the jewel in the crown of the council. Victorian Kingstown rightly regarded the baths as an indispensable heart of their deservedly popular seaside resort.

Propriety was observed: there was mixed bathing, but pools were separated by a heavy curtain – it disappeared suddenly one day in the 1930s. Separation of the sexes was the norm in Victorian times and strict local authority bye-laws applied to public bathing. There were hot baths and seaweed baths, which were open all year round. The baths were extremely popular with children and families, with cheap season tickets and rail fare offers. Excellent management by the dedicated staff, an attractive on-site restaurant and other facilities, which included comfortable dressing boxes for both ladies and gentlemen, all made the baths a national attraction.

Records of the local authority show how the baths were a major part of their operations and highlight the value of the premises themselves. There was, for example, a laundry on site, where 'towels were washed and dried thus ensuring perfect disinfectant and spotless cleaning'. Many people remember with great affection the happy times they had, over the years, enjoying the sea baths of Dún Laoghaire.

Sandycove Baths

John D'Alton tells us that 'commodious hot and cold water baths' were located in Sandycove. In 1838, Mr John Walsh was the proprietor of baths here, which became the Sandcove Ladies' Baths. In 1863, the Kingstown township purchased the baths with the Dublin Port and Docks Board. It was a small bathing place, with simple arrangements for easy handling, mostly frequented by children and families. However, the baths began to fall into disrepair, despite the pleadings of the Baths' Superintendent, Mr McKim, who had repeatedly sought funds for repair and refurbishment. In 1958, he reported to the Corporation 'that the baths were not fit to reopen' (after the winter). They closed in the early 1970s. The Curragh Sub-Aqua Club now have a lease of the premises.

The IASA, also concerned about the need for action, had been pressing the local authority since 1928, making helpful suggestions for a new Dún Laoghaire 'natatorium'. In 1937, the authority held a competition, for which twenty-five designs were received. The successful architects were Messrs Boyd Barrett, who had designed excellent baths for the sheltered Sandycove site. A coastal walkway and miniature railway on the seafront to Bullock Harbour were also proposed. Unfortunately, the outbreak of the Second World War resulted in postponement of the proposal, despite earlier government approval and Bord Fáilte endorsement. The postponement turned out to be permanent, as the plans for arguably the best site in Ireland never resurfaced at the end of the war.

Homan's of Killiney

In the 1800s, seawater baths were built in a small cottage on Killiney beach by the owners of Ayesha Castle (then called Victoria Castle). Extensive facilities followed with an indoor dance hall and tea rooms, now closed. The remains may be seen, standing over the beach on pillars. Seven single-roomed chalets were built in the early 1900s and were rented out to visitors, some from England, many of whom would return each summer. Homan's of Killiney was very popular with club outings and is remembered with great affection by many. The chalets were rented out until the mid-1950s. Teas and sandwiches continued to be served at summer weekends until the mid-1980s.

The World-Famous 'Forty Foot'

Also known locally as 'the Golden Years Advice Bureau', the 'Forty Foot', which is referred to in the first chapter of *Ulysses*, while not strictly baths, does share many of the characteristics and is still going strong. The army had an early presence here, probably establishing the tradition of an all-male bathing place. Records show that swimming was popular here in 1849, and races to Bullock Harbour and back were reported. Since 1880, the Forty Foot has been very well run by the Sandycove Bathers' Association (SBA) and its popularity continues to this day. The SBA is a voluntary, non-profit group under licence from the Minister of Finance and is funded by voluntary subscriptions. Despite the notice at the entrance, it is no longer confined to 'Gentlemen Only' – all are now welcome, provided, of course they behave themselves!

I like these lines by the late L.A. Strong:

Where are the men I worshiped then?
Some still rub the pink flesh dry,
Some have laid their towels by,
Some go by the tower still,
And some are passed to Hy-Brassil,
Where Fawcitt, he that dived and died,
Now plunges in a fairer tide.

References and Further Reading

Joyce, Weston St John, *The Neighbourhood of Dublin* (1994).

Laffan, Moira, *Frascati and the Lord Edward Fitzgerald Connection* (1999).

Lucas, A.T., *Washing and Bathing in Ancient Ireland* (1965).

Mac Coil, Liam, *The Book of Blackock* (1977).

O'Malley, Mary Pat, '*Lios an Uisce*' – The History of a House and its Occupants (1753-present day) (1982).

Ó Súilleabháin, Donal, *Ó Kingstown go Dún Laoghaire* (1976).

O'Sullivan, John & Cannon, Seamus, (eds), *The Book of Dún Laoghaire* (1987).

Pearson, Peter, *Between the Mountains and the Sea* (1998).

Pearson, Peter, *Dún Laoghaire–sKingston* (1981).

Sandymount Community Services, *The Road to Seapoint, Irishtown, and Ringsend* (1996).

This is Dublin – Official Guide (1962).

9

The Eighteenth-century Pirates of the Muglins

By Pádraig Laffan (1989)

For most of us with an interest in local history, it is the reference by Weston St John Joyce, in his book *The Neighbourhood of Dublin* (first published in 1912, and more recently reprinted in 1988 and again in 1994) that gives us our knowledge of an association between the Dalkey Islands and pirates. Let me quote it to you:

> To the N. E. is the group of rocks known as the 'Muglins' on which, in 1766, were hung in chains the bodies of the pirates Mackinley and Gidley who were executed for the murder of Capt. Cochrane, Capt. Glass and other passengers of the ship *Sandwich* on the high seas in the previous year.

If you sail past Dalkey Island with a friendly yachtsman, he will probably point out the Muglins, with the strange white conical beacon, 30 feet tall, with its red band and a flashing red light. This is the southern tip of Dublin Bay. He will give you the same five-line description that Joyce does, and no more, but there is a story there and I will tell it to you.

The lighthouse on the South Wall.

Captain George Glas

The first character in my narrative is Captain George Glas, although some accounts wrongly refer to him as Richard Glas. He is the most interesting person in the whole story. He was born in Dundee, Scotland, in 1725, the son of the Scottish Sectary (a religious minister), John Glas. He qualified as a surgeon and made many voyages to the West Indies as a ship's surgeon. According to one account, he was once a midshipman in the Royal Navy. It seems, however, that he accumulated some fortune on his voyages, and with this he bought a ship and appointed himself Captain.

One account of his life claims that he operated as a privateer, and that within days of sailing he had to quell a mutiny. This, the most colourful depiction of his life, attributes to him the capture of a rich French merchant-man, and claims that the loot from this ship pacified the mutinous crew. It goes on to say that they were later challenged by a French frigate of superior strength. He accepted the challenge and cleared the decks for action. The battle raged for two hours, with the privateer giving as good as she got until a second French warship appeared. Glas realised his situation was hopeless, and with half his crew dead or wounded, and himself shot through the shoulder, he surrendered. He was taken to the West Indies, where he was imprisoned and spent a considerable time in great hardship. Eventually, he was exchanged and secured his liberty. He then purchased another ship, which he also lost. This particular account claims that he went on to sail on other merchant ships plying to the West Indies, and suffered imprisonment no fewer than seven times in the wars that then raged. He always managed to be rescued or bought out.

The Great Settlement Plan of Captain George Glas

Glas obtained command of a vessel on the Brazil trade, and made several voyages to the west coast of Africa and the Canary Islands. However exaggerated some accounts of his career may be, he certainly was a resourceful man. On one of his trips he discovered a river between Cape Verde and Senegal, navigable some way inland, and came to the conclusion that it would be a suitable site for a new trading settlement, called Port Hillsborough. This was probably in the Western Sahara. He returned home to London and laid his scheme before the government, demanding exclusive trade rights for thirty years. These terms were considered excessive, but after some considerable negotiations, Glas came to an agreement with the Commissioners of Trade and Plantations, by which he was guaranteed the sum of £15,000 on condition that he obtain free cession of the country by the natives to the British Crown. On faith of this arrangement, Glas entered into an agreement with a firm of merchants who provided him with a ship and cargo. There are details of his agreement with the government in the calendar of Home Office Papers, 1760-1765.

The Canary Islands

In 1764, he published a book, which may be seen in the National Library in Dublin, entitled *The History of the Discovery and Conquest of the Canary Islands* (translated from a Spanish manuscript lately found in the island of Palma, attributed to J. Abreu de Galinda, Franciscan monk). In the book, Glas not only enquires into the origins of the ancient inhabitants of the Canary Islands, but also gives an account of the modern history of the islands and a description of the inhabitants. At the time of his death, he had a project underway to publish a history 'of that part of Africa bounded on the West by the Atlantic Ocean and on the East by Nubia and Abbesinnia' (Sudan and Ethiopia).

But back to the story.

Glas sailed from Gravesend in August 1764, accompanied by his wife and daughter, and arrived safely at his destination, which he named Port Hillsborough. There was a famine prevailing at that time in this part of Africa and this may have facilitated his efforts. He persuaded the natives to cede their territory, and a treaty was drawn up and signed by the headmen of the district. Glas resolved to proceed to Tenerife to obtain grain and other provisions for his settlement. He was obliged to leave the ship with his companions, as they had no place ashore to stay and, I suspect, were uncertain of their security in that place. Leaving his wife and child, he set out in the longboat with five men in November 1764. He arrived safely in Lanzarote in the Canaries, where an English vessel was on the point of sailing home and by which he forwarded his treaty to the authorities in London. But the jealousy of the Spaniards was, by this time, aroused and, shortly afterwards, Glas was arrested on a charge of contraband trading and sent as a prisoner to Tenerife, where he was treated with great harshness.

Among the Home Office papers is a letter from Mr George Glas, dated Tenerife, 15 December 1764, reporting his seizure and close confinement. He suggests that the Spaniards feared interference with the important fishery carried on by the Canary Islanders on the African coast between Cape Bojador and Cape Blanco, and asks that they obtain his release. Other letters to the admiralty, from Captain Graves of HMS *Edgar* off Senegal, 22 March 1765, and from Captain Boteler of HMS *Shannon*, confirm the strictness of his detention and the claim by the Spanish of contrabanding.

About the same time, the settlers of Port Hillsborough were attacked by the natives, who killed the Chief Officer and six men. The survivors made their escape and sailed to Tenerife, where Mrs Glas first learned of her husband's detention. Steps appear to have been taken by the British Government to obtain his release and in October of 1765 he was set free. The English barque *Sandwich* or *Earl of Sandwich* called at Tenerife, and Glas and his wife and daughter embarked for England.

The *Sandwich*: A True Treasure Ship

There are other reports which say that Glas was in partnership with Captain Cochrane of the Sandwich. Whatever their connection, the Sandwich had sailed from London in July 1765 with bale goods and hardware for Santa Cruz and, thence, to Oratairia in the Canary Islands, where she took on board a cargo of Madeira wine, raw and manufactured silk, cochineal (dried bodies of the female insect *Dactylopius coccus*, found on cacti and used for making red dye), and a large quantity of Spanish milled dollars, some ingots of gold, some jewels and a small quantity of gold dust. She was truly a treasure ship. When the *Earl of Sandwich* sailed for London in November 1765, there were on board: Captain Glas, Mrs Glas, their daughter, and their servant boy, not named. The crew of the ship were John Cochrane (the captain), Charles Pinechent (the mate), Peter McKinlie (the bosun), George Gidley (the cook), Richard St Quinten, Andera Zekerman, James Pinechent (the mate's brother), and Benjamin Gallipsey (the cabin boy).

Murder Most Foul

George Gidley and Richard St Quinten, both West of England men, conspired with Peter McKinlie, an Irishman, and Andreas Zekerman, a Dutchman, to take over the ship, dispose of those on board and seize the treasure.

On the night of Sunday, 30 November, McKinlie and Gidley were on night watch when Captain Cochrane, returning to his cabin, was seized by McKinlie, who held him while Gidley beat him to death with an iron bar. The noise of the scuffle and the groans of the Captain awoke the Pinechents – the mate and his brother – who came on deck only to be surprised, tripped and thrown overboard along with Captain Cochrane. Captain Glas, on his way on deck, ran back to his cabin and armed himself with his sword. He would be a more formidable opponent. McKinlie spotted this and hid at the foot of the steps in the dark, and, as Glas came out, he leaped on him and held him, shouting for the others. Zekerman came running and managed to get the sword from Glas, incurring a stab wound before he succeeded. Equipped with the sword, he ran Glas through, and in the process stabbed McKinlie in the arm. The unfortunate Glas, overcome by numbers, succumbed and was thrown overboard.

Then McKinlie and Zekerman went for Mrs Glas and found her on the poop deck. She pleaded for mercy, and as they later admitted, cried, 'If you won't spare me, surely so small as her has done you no harm, spare my little one' and hugged the child to her. 'To the Devil with you and your child,' was McKinlie's answer, and he threw the unfortunate woman overboard with the child still in her arms. Only the cabin boy, Benjamin Gallipsey, and the Glas family servant boy remained.

The ship was now in the Bristol Channel *en route* to London. Course was changed for Ireland and, on Tuesday 3 December at about 2 p.m., they arrived about twelve leagues off Waterford. They prepared to scuttle the ship. The longboat was hoisted out and loaded with about two tons of booty, bags of dollars, jewels and gold. They opened the ballast seacocks. As the boat pulled away, the two boys pleaded to be taken. One jumped into the sea, swam to the boat and grabbed hold of the gunwhales. They hit him until he fell back into the water and drowned. The other boy, still on the ship, with sails still set and rolling heavily as she filled, was in a panic and, losing his hold, fell overboard and disappeared.

Landfall Waterford

The longboat reached Waterford Harbour and went upriver to a point about two miles from Duncannon, near Broomhill. Here, they landed and buried most of the treasure at half ebb, 250 bags of it. They hid more in holes in the rocks near the sea. Then they set off again upriver, taking what they would be able to carry, and landed at Fisherstown, four miles from New Ross. They went to an ale house at a village called Ballybrazil; they overindulged and were robbed of 1,300 dollars.

On 4 December, they went to New Ross, where they put up in an alehouse and exchanged 1,200 Spanish dollars for current gold. They bought three cases of pistols. In their first accommodation, they called the landlady upstairs and bade her light a fire and dry their goods for them as they were wet through. This landlady's eyes must have opened wide in surprise, as in the song, when she saw what was to be dried. They gave her a present of a necklace, earrings and a snuffbox, and to her maid, similar gifts and money. Some of the villains were much cut about the face and there were two who had stab wounds. These injuries, they claimed, were inflicted by pirates whom they had encountered during a voyage from Mexico and from whom they had barely managed to escape. Nonetheless, suspicions were aroused. Six horses and two guides were hired and the four set out for Dublin, where they arrived on 6 December and lodged in The Bull in Thomas Street.

Ghost Ship

The fate of the four free-spending sailors took another twist, when, dressed above their station and scarred with injuries, they came to the attention of local reporters. Here's what the *Public Gazetter*, a newspaper of the time, reported:

6 December Waterford

Last Wednesday at about 6 o'clock came in Captain Honewell from Newfoundland, about four leagues to the Southwest of the tower he had like to run foul of a large three-masted vessel. The weather was hazy which prevented him seeing her. Her top gallant yards were up and she was so deep in the water that he could only see her rails. She had no boat nor could a living creature be seen. Eight boats went out to investigate but the weather was too bad.

The report goes on to describe numbers of pipes of wine being driven ashore on the island of Cain, the estate of Mr Wyse, 'One hogshead of refined sugar containing 808lbs dated 5 August 1765 marked O in a diamond, shipped by one Blye on the *Earl of Sandwich* One Cochrane Master for the Canaries.'

This account also mentions four tolerably well-dressed men having stayed in the public house in Ross, and their gifts, and that the landlady sewed up twelve bags of dollars for them. It also notes that two of the men were much cut about the face. Finally, the rest of the ship came ashore.

Justice

The collector of Ross examined the wreckage and sent two express messengers to the Chief Magistrate of Ross, who was then in Dublin, asking him to arrest the men on suspicion of felony. Meanwhile, back in Dublin, McKinlie sold £300 worth of Spanish dollars to a goldsmith who became suspicious and followed him to his lodging and informed the authorities.

St Quinten and Zekerman were arrested and lodged at Newgate, whilst McKinlie and Gidley escaped. The first two confessed to the crime and revealed the whereabouts of McKinlie, who was also captured. He, in turn, informed the authorities that Gidley had left by post chaise for Cork, *en route* to England. The Magistrate of Ross sent messengers with orders to the collector there and also to the officer commanding the fort at Duncannon, directing them to recover the buried bags of treasure and to secure them.

Going south, the messengers overtook Gidley. He was taken at the Royal Garter in Castledermot. They arrested him and lodged him in Carlow Gaol. He was dressed in a coat of blue laced with gold, said to have belonged to Captain Glas, and carried on his person fifty-three guineas, a gold *moidore* (a Portuguese gold coin) and also a quantity of silver. He had agreed to pay twelve guineas for his post-chaise-and-four to Cork. A few days later, 250 bags of dollars were recovered from the hiding place and brought under guard to New Ross custom house. When captured, the other three prisoners were found to be carrying gold, gold dust and ingots.

Trial and Punishment

The trial took place in Dublin in March 1776. The court was packed and hundreds filled the street, causing a complete stoppage of traffic. The *Freeman's Journal* reported as follows:

> On Saturday, 1st inst. came on at the commission of Oyer and Terminer the trials of Andreas Zekerman, Richard St Quinten, George Gidley and Peter McKinlie, who murdered Captain Cochrane, late Commander of the ship *The Earl of Sandwich*, Captain Glass, his wife and daughter and others on board ship, and sunk her. When they were found guilty yesterday, they were executed at St Stephen's Green. They were attended at the place of execution by a strong military guard consisting of horse and foot. The bodies were carried back to Newgate, there to remain to be hung in chains as may be appointed.

And indeed it was so appointed. The bodies were brought in the black cart from Newgate to be hung in the most conspicuous places in Poolbeg; two near McCarill's Wharf, on the south wall, and the other two about the middle of the piles below the Pigeon House.

People taking walks began to complain about the sight and the 'atmosphere', and indeed also that the metal hoops containing the bodies were imperfect. Letters to the papers complained particularly of the quality of the hanging irons.

A Warning to Sailors

On 1 April 1766, the *Freeman's Journal* reported that the body of McKinlie 'fell from the gibbet on the south wall', and that it and the body of Gidley were to be removed to be hung in new irons on Dalkey Island. Those of Zekerman and St Quinten were to remain in the piles at the Pigeon House. The last report on the matter was to say that the two bodies were removed to Dalkey Island and there fixed in the new irons, which were said to be 'the compleatest ever made in this kingdom'.

And so it was that McKinlie and Gidley became known as the Pirates of Dalkey or of the Muglins, where their gibbet was finally set.

They were not strictly pirates – really mutineers, or what we today would call hijackers. No one, to my knowledge, was ever executed on the Dalkey Islands and no pirates ever had their base there.

If you are after treasure, consider this: as the villains came ashore in the longboat from the sinking ship they threw a large quantity of dollars overboard to lighten the boat. What about the booty hidden in the rocks?

Dalkey Island and the Muglins beyond.

A The South
Wall and B the
Muglins on
Taylor's Map,
1816.

My last words on this are to invite you to read a notice
inserted in the *Dublin Gazette* of Tuesday 4 March 1766:

> Booley Bay in the County of Wexford, the place where
> the treasure (alleged to have been taken out of the ship *The
> Earl of Sandwich*) was lately found, is the estate of the Rt
> Hon. Lord Viscount Loftus of Ely to whom all the royalties,
> treasure trove, etc., belong. The same being granted by the
> Crown to his Lordships Ancestors and his heirs forever.

The viscount expected the sea to yield more. Some of it
is still there somewhere.

References and Further Reading

Dún Laoghaire Borough Times, NLI.
Freeman's Journal, December 1765–April 1776, NLI.
Gentleman's Magazine, XXXV 545, NLI.
Glas, George, *The History of the Discovery and Conquest of the Canary
Islands* (translated from a manuscript of J. Abreu de Galinda, a
franciscan monk), NLI.

London Chronicle, 1766, NLI.
Public Gazetter, Dublin, August 1765-September 1770, NLI.

Addenda

Wright, G.N., *Historical Guide to the City of Dublin* (1825):

POLICING: The first institution of police in Dublin is
said to have taken place in the reign of Elizabeth; to this
succeeded a class of peace preservers and night guards called
watchmen, who were introduced in the reign of George
I. The watchmen were not very successful, many of them
being convicted of aiding in robberies and murder. This led
Mr Orde to introduce the Police Act of 1785. This body
was quite efficient, but much resented by the citizens. Many
attempts were made in parliament to repeal the Police Act.
It was eventually repealed in 1795, and the miserable system
of watch restored. About twelve years later, the Duke of
Wellington, the Secretary of State in Ireland, introduced the
Police Act, which brought about policing as we know it.

PRISONS: The principal gaol for all malefactors was in
Green Street. Formerly, the gaol was an old castle on the
town wall over the gate leading from Cut Purse Row to
Thomas Street, and from its situation derived the name,
'Newgate', which appellation was transferred to the
subsequent prison, built in 1773 and opened in 1781. This
building, on a rectangular piece of ground after a design of
Thomas Cooley, was a three-storey building. In front of the
upper storey was the platform and apparatus of execution.

10

Samuel Beckett:
Early Days in Foxrock

by Noelle Ryan (1982)

Samuel Beckett was born on 13 April 1906, in Cooldrinagh, which is on Brighton Road at the junction of Kerrymount Avenue. It was Good Friday. William, his father, who was born in Dublin, was a quantity surveyor in the family business of building contractors. His mother, May, came from Leixlip, County Kildare. Her father, Samuel Roe, was the owner of a grain mill in Leixlip.

Cooldrinagh is an imposing, Tudor-style residence set attractively in the middle of several acres facing the Wicklow Hills. It was built in 1903 for William Beckett by Frederick Hicks, a leading architect and president of the Architectural Association of Ireland at that time. A photograph and blueprint of the house was featured, shortly after it was built, in the *Irish Builder*, an important trade publication.

For one who lived all his adult life with such frugality and self-denial, Samuel Beckett had a surprisingly comfortable and conventional upbringing. When asked some years ago if he had had a happy childhood, he replied, 'It was uneventful;

you might say it was a happy childhood, although I had little talent for happiness. My parents did everything that could make a child happy, but I was often lonely.'

Family Life

From the beginning of his development, Beckett's mother was determined to conquer Samuel's stubbornness and his refusal to be reached. He was just as determined to maintain his independence from her domination. This battle of wills continued, through periods of rage and depression, throughout Mrs Beckett's lifetime.

There were two sons in the Beckett family, Samuel and Frank, who was four years senior. They were very close, although Samuel seemed the elder, as he was always the leader in their games and exploits. They went bird-nesting in the vacant fields across from Cooldrinagh and played bicycle polo on a neighbour's tennis court. There was special emphasis placed on outdoor activities. Their father went swimming regularly with the boys in the Forty Foot, and went for long walks in the Dublin Mountains.

Beckett the Sportsman

William Beckett was secretary of Carrickmines Golf Club, and when Samuel Beckett was older he accompanied his father to the club on Sunday afternoons. I am informed firsthand by a man still resident in Foxrock, who played golf with Samuel Beckett at Carrickmines when they were both students at Trinity College, that he was a good, but most unorthodox, golfer. He never had more than four golf clubs and putted with a No.2 iron.

He has also been described as a brilliant – though flashy – cricket player, with some very stylish strokes. Cricket fans will find it intriguing that Beckett batted left-handed and bowled right-handed. Boxing also entered into his sporting repertoire, and during his time in Portora School he became light heavyweight champion. His father was delighted with this achievement, as he had always prodded his sons towards physical well-being and athletic excellence.

On Sunday mornings, Mrs Beckett and the boys walked the short distance from Cooldrinagh to Tullow parish church, where they owned a pew. Beatrice Orpen, who was then a prominent painter in Dublin, sat with her family in a pew opposite the Becketts and remembered Sam frowning at her, week after week. She discovered that his dissatisfaction was nothing personal, 'it was towards the whole cosmos rather than me in particular'.

In 1914, when Samuel was eight years old, three children of Mrs Beckett's brother Edward Price Roe, whose wife had died, came to live at Cooldrinagh. Mollie was thirteen, Sheila eleven, and Jack nine, and they remained there until they were adults. There were now five children in the Beckett family.

Schooldays

Samuel Beckett's education began when he was five years old at the private academy of Miss Ida Elsnor. She and her sister, two elderly German spinsters, operated a kindergarten from their home in Leopardstown. When Beckett wrote his novel *Molloy*, he immortalised them. Then he went to Earlsfort House School, 4 Earlsfort Place. The school was founded by Alfred Le Peton, who was a professor of French. So Beckett had a bilingual education from the beginning of his studies in this school. Each day saw Frank and Samuel ride their bicycles to Foxrock railway station, now unfortunately abandoned. (Foxrock is referred to as 'Boghill' in Beckett's radio play *All That Fall*.) There they boarded the Dublin and South Eastern Railway (dubbed 'the slow and easy' by the boys) to Harcourt Street.

He left Earlsfort House School in 1919, and in the Easter term of 1920, he followed his brother to Portora Royal in Enniskillen. Oscar Wilde was another famous pupil of this school. His name was removed from the awards roll subsequent to the scandal with Lord Alfred Douglas, but it has happily been reinstated. Beckett excelled himself athletically, but his academic achievements were not so impressive. Portora left no lasting impression on him, nor does he remember his time there with fondness. While his many kindnesses and generous responses to appeals from Trinity are well known, he did not respond to one single appeal from Portora.

Trinity College Days

He entered Trinity College in October 1923. He continued to live at home for his first two years at the university. He dabbled in various courses but he eventually decided on Modern Languages. At the conclusion of his third year, he came fourth in his class and received a foundation scholarship in Modern Languages. His athletic career also prospered but it took second place.

About this time, Beckett became involved with the artistic, or bohemian, circle of the university. He became a visitor at Madame Cogley's, a pub near Trinity College. Madame Cogley was a Frenchwoman married to an Irishman. She had literary pretensions and welcomed a clientele who had the same ambitions. Pádraig Ó Conaire, the Galway poet famed for drinking his stout laced with black pepper, was often there, as were Liam O'Flaherty, Austin Clarke and Louis MacNeice.

Davy Byrne's was another Beckett favourite. Here he met people like Cecil Salkeld (who was to become father-in-law to Brendan Behan), Brindsley McNamara and Francis McNamara (who was to become father-in-law to Dylan Thomas).

The theatre began to take the place of cricket and other sports as Beckett's favourite pastime. Dublin was bursting with theatre in 1920. Sean O'Casey, Lennox Robinson and Lady Gregory thrilled audiences at the Abbey Theatre, and Beckett was among them on several of O'Casey's first nights. He saw there a different sort of society than he had known in Foxrock.

At the Queen's Theatre he developed a lifelong passion for slapstick. The Gate at that time was the home of experimental European drama, and the Abbey the home of Irish nationalism. The difference between the Gate and the Abbey was described by a wit of the day as being the difference between 'Sodom and Begorrah'. The curious thing about Beckett's theatre-going was that it was solitary. He seemed to have studied the works he saw as much – or more – than he enjoyed them.

During this time, he became more withdrawn from the Foxrock world, and his father's talk of business and sport. He and Frank still played tennis and took long, silent walks on the Glencullen Road from the back of the Pine Forest to Sally Gap. This was Beckett's favourite walk in all of Ireland, and one which he described repeatedly in his later writings.

His remoteness towards his family became more marked and the closeness he had had with his brother in earlier life disappeared. Frank had graduated from Trinity and was working with his father. It had been hoped that Samuel would also join the family business, but he began to give them hints this would not happen.

He started drinking; careered madly about the countryside in the Wicklow Hills on his motorbike. He was a reckless driver and had been involved in several serious accidents, ruining his machine but not seriously harming himself. His mother had rigid ideas

Cooldrinagh, Samuel Beckett's home in Foxrock.

about suitable companions and proper conduct, and she disapproved strongly of this behaviour, the people who were his friends, and the parties he attended.

Some of his Trinity friends were welcome at Cooldrinagh, but other friends, members of the artistic or bohemian circle, were considered not to be the right sort, and his mother's displeasure was evident. Rumours of his erratic behaviour were a matter of grave concern to his parents. However, on 8 December 1927, he stood first in his class, and received his BA degree in Modern Languages and a gold medal for outstanding scholarship.

Life in Paris

The only writing he had done up until then had been more scholarly than creative. Then, in 1928, he began two years as lecturer at École Normale Supérieur in Paris, which changed the direction of his life. This famous and distinguished institution boasted among its lecturers Jean Paul Sartre and Simone Veil, President of the European Parliament.

While at Trinity, Beckett had become an ardent devotee of James Joyce, who was then living in Paris. Beckett paid him a visit and became his friend. He also became his assistant for a time.

In 1931, Beckett returned to Dublin, where he was made a lecturer in French at Trinity College. He took his MA, but he became impatient with teaching and with life in Dublin, and soon resigned his lectureship to devote his time to writing.

War

He was in Ireland when the Second World War broke out. He left immediately for France, where he later became an activist for the French resistance. He also worked at a field hospital run by the Irish Red Cross at St-Lô in Normandy. He was awarded the *Croix de Guerre* for his work in the resistance movement.

After the war, Beckett made another visit to Ireland. He remained for a time with his mother at Cooldrinagh. Each year after this, until her death in 1950, he spent a month in Ireland.

The return and departure were proving to be equally painful. His father had died in 1933. This upset him greatly, as his father had been very dear to him. William Beckett had given his love wholeheartedly, even though he had no real understanding of his son. But the greater part of Samuel Beckett's time was now spent in Paris, writing in French.

Local References

His fascination for his country of adoption remained with him, but he had not completely rejected his ethnic origins. He still maintained an Irish passport. There was a marked Irishness in the names of some of his main characters: Molloy, Malone, Lynch and Kelly.

There were frequent references to Irish place names and subject matter in his work, a few examples of which are:
1. Cooldrinagh referred to in *How It Is*. 'We are on a veranda smothered in verbena; the scented sun dapples the red tiles.'

2. Foxrock railway station, as already mentioned, is remembered as Boghill in radio play *All That Fall*. At the station, Tommy the porter and Mr Slocum, clerk of nearby Leopardstown Racecourse, discuss the Ladies' Plate that is to be run that day, and a horse called Flash Harry. Mr Slocum tips the horse to win the race.

3. In his first English novel, called *Watt*, the geography of south County Dublin, the leadworks, the racecourse, Leopardstown, and the mental hospital St John of God's, Stillorgan, are all mentioned.

In 1969, Beckett won the Nobel Prize for Literature. He was a bit uneasy, as he felt that Joyce deserved it more but had never won it. He had left Paris for a remote village in Tunisia to escape the publicity, and in a letter to a friend he wrote, 'My only regret is that I cannot properly celebrate because there is no Irish here, only Vat 69.'

The Nobel Prize was the ultimate recognition of his genius, and in years to come, when he has joined the other Anglo-Irish immortals, Yeats and Joyce, and when summer schools are arranged in his honour, devotees will find numerous places of pilgrimage within a convenient distance of Dublin. In *Ulysees*, Joyce relates Mr Bloom's journey to identifiable landmarks in the city. There is, too, I think, for those who seek it, a Beckett Country that ranges over South Dublin, centred in his native area of Foxrock.